Tales of
Old Middlesex

Other counties in this series include:

Tales of
Old Middlesex

Mike Hall

With illustrations by Catherine Hall

COUNTRYSIDE BOOKS
NEWBURY, BERKSHIRE

First published 2001
© Mike Hall 2001

COUNTRYSIDE BOOKS
3 Catherine Road
Newbury, Berkshire

To view our complete range of books,
please visit us at
www.countrysidebooks.co.uk

ISBN 1 85306 701 6

Cover illustration by Colin Doggett

Produced through MRM Associates Ltd., Reading
Printed by J. W. Arrowsmith Ltd., Bristol

For my wife, Linda, and daughters,
Catherine and Elizabeth

Contents

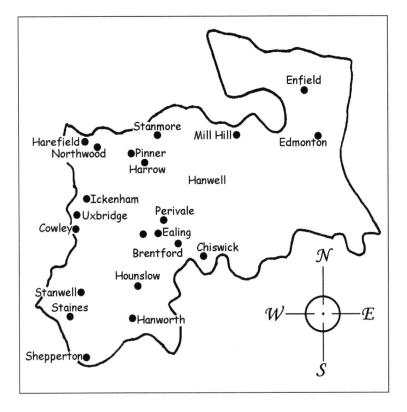

Acknowledgements

THE research for this collection has taken me all round the old county of Middlesex and I am grateful to the library staff and members of local history societies who have given me assistance.

Old topographical books on Middlesex, of the type that do not seem to be produced now, often set me off on the trail of some forgotten anecdote. The Middlesex volume in Arthur Mee's *King's England* series, *Middlesex* by Michael Robins (1953), *Middlesex Old & New* by Martin S. Briggs (1934) and *Highways and Byways in Middlesex* (1909) were among the most useful. The first volume of Edward Walford's *Greater London* (1882–4) introduced me to a number of tales described in wonderfully verbose detail. Of modern works, the series on Middlesex districts published by Historical Publications Ltd (notably *Southgate and Edmonton Past* by Graham Dalling) have been very useful.

The Haunted Windmill of Perivale

∾

HIDDEN away from the roaring traffic on Western Avenue and the factories of the trading estate, Perivale's tiny rustic church with its weather-boarded tower survives from the time when the village was one of Middlesex's smallest and most remote.

There was an old windmill too – home, according to legend, of a notorious miser in the early years of the 17th century.

Villagers told how the mill was haunted by the ghost of the miller and an evil witch who had cursed him. A struggle had followed and the witch had fallen to her death from the mill ladder. This had done the miller no good at all though: he was found crushed to death between his own millstones.

The mill then decayed into a ruinous condition. No one dared disturb its dusty floors and sinisterly creaking wooden walls for fear of what they might find. Then a notorious old miser saw the opportunity to make a good investment by purchasing the derelict building. Perhaps he wanted to secrete his bags of money in its lofts where nobody would risk breaking in to steal them.

Time went on and after a while the people of Perivale realised that no one had seen the old man for months. Had something perhaps happened to him? What had become of his money?

They agreed that somebody should brave the terrors of the haunted mill to go and find out – but no one dared. Everyone asked made the excuse that they had a wife, children or aged parents to support. 'What would become of them if anything happened to me?' they reasoned.

But there was a young man in the village who was a foundling, an orphan, a man with no family. His name was Simon Coston. 'You could do it,' they said.

Simon looked nervous but allowed himself to be persuaded. Squaring his shoulders he entered the darkened mill at the ground floor and was then heard slowly climbing the creaky stairs. Suddenly his anguished face appeared at the gallery at the top of the windmill: 'The ghost! The ghost!' he cried. 'Flee for your lives!'

The watchers needed no further warning. They scattered and fled to their cottages across the fields. Hours later, and fortified by copious amounts of strong ale, a few brave souls returned to the mill. They did indeed find the body of the old miser – but of his moneybags and of young Simon Coston there was no trace at all!

And somehow, when the poor foundling returned to Perivale, he had come into money. Indeed there was cash enough to endow the church with a fine font cover of carved oak. It is still there because when in 1836 there was a proposal to replace both font and cover with something more modern and stylish, the idea was turned down by the villagers.

The excuse they gave then was 'because there are no christenings for parishioners of Perivale, nor likely to be any' – but the real reason may be that the ghost of that same Simon Coston, who died in about 1666, was still believed to stalk the lanes on dark nights, just like the miller and the witch before him.

Perhaps they still do.

Saucy Scandal
at
Royal Hanworth

❧

HANWORTH is today an unremarkable suburb under the flightpaths into Heathrow Airport. An unlikely setting for scandal and intrigue touching on the royal family, you might think, but not in Tudor times.

The young Princess Elizabeth, a 14 year old at the time of her father Henry VIII's death and the accession of the young Edward VI as King in 1547, was in the care of his last wife, Catherine Parr, who had palaces at both Chelsea and Hanworth. In many ways Catherine was an ideal stepmother, one of the most educated women of the time. She encouraged Elizabeth's love of study and her flair for languages and procured the services of the best tutors to further her education.

Young Elizabeth was turning into quite a beauty – auburn haired with an intelligent face and innocent childlike eyes. This could, however, have been her downfall for she attracted the attentions of the unscrupulous 40 year old Lord Thomas Seymour, whose brother

Edward, a trusted confidant of the late King, had seized supreme political power to become Protector during the years of the boy King's minority.

Edward Seymour was well aware of the personal vices and shortcomings of his brother. He appointed him to the titular position of Lord High Admiral but denied him any real power. Thomas, meanwhile, plotted to oust his brother and, as a stepping stone to this ambition, married the Queen Dowager, Catherine.

He used his position in Catherine's household to flirt brazenly with the teenage Princess in a way that eventually led the jealous Catherine, by now pregnant, to banish Elizabeth to the care of Sir Anthony Denny at Cheshunt in Hertfordshire. Sir Anthony was brother-in-law to Elizabeth's nurse and Keeper of the Wardrobe, Kate Ashley, and it was she who gave damning testimony against the Lord High Admiral when his intrigues and scheming for power became too much. He was sent to the Tower and arraigned before the Privy Council in 1549. By this time Catherine had died in childbirth and the old reprobate had expressed the wish to marry Elizabeth – 'Nay, it is but London news,' was her blunt reply to rumours that she was still fond of him. The Admiral's plans by now included a scheme to kidnap King Edward and marry him to his ward, Lady Jane Grey, who had her own claim to the throne.

At Seymour's trial for treason Kate recalled how he would steal kisses from the 14 year old Elizabeth, smack her and take the key of her bedroom. On one occasion in the gardens at Hanworth, she alleged, he had cut the black dress that Elizabeth was wearing into a hundred pieces while Queen Catherine held her. The Queen Dowager and the Lord Admiral would come and tickle her in bed. Then he started coming in alone!

Some mornings, Kate continued, Seymour would come into the bedroom uninvited 'before she was ready and sometimes before she did rise. If she were up he would bid her good morrow and ask how she did. He would strike her upon the back or on the buttocks familiarly. And if she were in bed he would open the curtains and bid her good morrow and make as though he could come at her, and she would go further in the bed so that he could not.'

She spoke of the morning Seymour tried to kiss her in bed but was scolded away by Kate herself. Another time Elizabeth, hearing his key in the lock, ran out of bed to hide behind the bed curtains, until he got tired of waiting for her. On yet another occasion Kate caught Seymour in Elizabeth's room in his nightgown! Elizabeth by now took good care to be up and dressed early.

For a time in 1549 the charges against Thomas Seymour threatened Elizabeth herself but although he was executed for high treason – partly for his attempts to seduce her into marriage – Elizabeth was spared but for a time she was in disgrace and her brother refused to receive her at court.

Elizabeth later described her erstwhile lover as 'a man of much wit and little judgement' but perhaps she had some fond memories of those illicit trysts in the chambers and gardens of the old palace at Hanworth. The attentions of an older, more experienced man might have been flattering for the young girl but the attraction had probably worn thin well before that last embrace that led Queen Catherine to banish her to Cheshunt. By now she had seen through his motives and the old roué with his tired jokes had become pathetic and repulsive.

SAUCY SCANDAL AT ROYAL HANWORTH

Elizabeth's memories of her time at Hanworth cannot, though, have been too traumatic for she revisited the park in 1600, when she was Queen, and hunted there.

How different our history would have been if Elizabeth had succumbed to those attentions. Perhaps it was at Hanworth that she realised the dangers posed by the sexual intrigues and passions to which her mother, Anne Boleyn, had fallen victim. She would not forget the Admiral, who had first inspired her love, but realised the real danger he had put her into. The Virgin Queen had learned her lesson.

The Wild-Eyed Vegan

❧

TODAY we celebrate the individual – to stand out from the crowd, to have your own fads and fetishes is almost compulsory if you want to get ahead in life. But it was bad form back in the 17th century when it was important to know what your lords and masters were preaching and to trim your beliefs accordingly!

Roger Crab was a vegetarian – nothing unusual in that today and even then it probably would not have got him into trouble if he had kept quiet about it but he just had to sound off on the subject in a series of printed tracts, the tabloid press of the day, that circulated in the streets and taverns of London.

They were not brief and to the point, these broadsheets. The one concerning Roger Crab began: 'The English Hermite, or Wonder of this Age – Being a Relation of the Life of Roger Crab, living near Uxbridge; taken from his own Mouth showing his strange, reserved and unparall'd Kind of Life who counted it a sin against his Body and Soule to eat any Sort of Flesh, Fish or Living Creature; or to drink any

Wine, Ale or Beere. He can live on three farthinges a Week. His constant Food is Roots and Hearbes, as Cabbages, Turneps, Carrots, Dock-Leaves and Grass, also Bread and Bran without Butter or Cheese. His Cloathing is Sack Cloath. He left the Army, and kept a Shop at Chesham, and now has left off that, and sold his considerable Estate to give to the Poore, shewing his Reasons from the Scripture.'

And that was just the title.

Ickenham today is a pleasant outer suburb, two stops before Uxbridge at the end of the Metropolitan and Piccadilly lines, but around the little church of St Giles, with its pretty timber bellcote, there is just a hint of the rural village it once was.

Back in 1651 when Roger Crab first arrived there the villagers must have found him very odd indeed. Like many who had 'got religion' later in life, he claimed to have previously lived a spectacularly wicked life. 'I have transgressed the commands of God,' he roared, 'and so am found guilty of the whole law, living in pride, drunkenness and gluttony, which I upheld by dissembling and lying, cheating and cozening my neighbours.'

Not the easiest of companions then, this wild-eyed veteran of the Parliamentary Army who still bore the scars of a severe head wound – 'I were cloven to the brain,' he told anyone who would listen.

And there were some who reckoned that bump on the head explained a lot!

Crab, however, blamed all the world's evil on the eating of meat and would not touch the stuff. The story went around Ickenham of how, during the war, he had persuaded a certain Captain Norwood to take up his rigorous diet. As the unfortunate captain had later died,

19

this did not seem to many to be a good advertisement for it.

You were wise not to argue, though. By the time he came to Ickenham he claimed to be 'above the Law, having a personal revelation of the paradise of God and having no sympathy with levellers, nor Quakers, nor Shakers nor ranters.'

Yet the proceeds of the sale of his hat shop in Chesham had gone to the poor and he had built his little cottage near St Giles' church with his own hands. He got a reputation as a physician and as an astrologer, foretelling the Restoration of Charles II long before the event.

But still he got into trouble. Twice he was summoned to appear before the Justices for Sabbath-breaking and when he came to London for the publication of *The English Hermite* in 1655 he found himself imprisoned in Clerkenwell. He complained that his jailer brought him nothing to eat – but then perhaps the poor man had never had to deal with such a fussy eater!

When he died in 1680 an anonymous epitaph writer, who must have known this strange visionary better than most, put these words above his grave:

Tread gently, reader, near the dust
Committed to this tomb-stone's trust;
For while 'twas flesh it held a guest
With universal love possest;
A soul that stemmed opinion's tide,
Did over sects in triumph ride;
Yet separate from the giddy crowd,
And paths traditions had allowed,
Through good and ill report he past
Oft censored, yet approved at last;

THE WILD-EYED VEGAN

Wouldst thou his religion know
In brief 'twas this; to all to do unto;
So in kind Nature's laws he stood
A temple undefiled with blood;
A friend to everything was good
The rest Angels alone can fitly tell,
Haste then to them, and Him, and so:
    Farewell.

The Mystery
of Cromwell's
Headless Corpse

❧

SOME say that the headless body of Oliver Cromwell, once Lord Protector of England, lies buried, not at the family home, but under a layer of concrete at St Nicholas' church, Chiswick.

When Cromwell died in 1658, having held supreme power for five years, his body was embalmed and buried in Westminster Abbey. His son Richard took his father's place. The revolutionary leadership had become hereditary.

But Richard was not the man his father was and the unsmiling rule of Parliament and the Puritans had become irksome. When the monarchy was restored to general acclamation in 1660, it was not likely that the body of the regicide Oliver Cromwell would remain undisturbed. In a display of officially-sanctioned vengeance the remains were dug up gleefully in January 1661. After spending a night under guard at the Red Lion Inn, Holborn, Cromwell's body was dragged through the streets of London to Tyburn. Still wrapped in its grave clothes, it was given a mock execution by hanging. Six hours later, the corpse was lowered from the gallows and clumsily beheaded, needing at least six blows of the axe to do the job. A few fingers, toes and an ear were cut off for individuals to keep as mementos. The head was then paraded in triumph through the streets, insults and rubbish were thrown at it and five days later it was prominently displayed in Westminster Hall, an iron-tipped pole driven through the top of the skull. There it remained for over twenty years as a macabre warning to any future rebels. The rest of the body was supposedly buried under the gallows but there were widespread and persistent rumours that Cromwell's children rescued it and spirited it away.

But why Chiswick?

Cromwell's daughter Mary loved her father dearly and was devastated when he died. What happened to his body later would have been repulsive to her. She was a formidable lady in her own right – some maintained that she would have made a much better successor in her father's role than Richard had done. Of the membership of Parliament she said once that 'those who wore the breeches would have suited petticoats better – but if those in petticoats had been in the breeches they would have held the faster!'

From 1676 until her death in 1713 this grand dame and patron of the arts lived with her then husband Lord Fauconberg at Sutton Court, Chiswick. She is buried in a vault inside the church, together with her sister, Lady Frances Russell.

When St Nicholas' church was rebuilt – somewhat controversially – in 1882, the Fauconberg vault was opened. Captain Dale, the son of the Vicar, saw this take place and thereafter claimed that there were not two coffins but three and that the third coffin appeared to have been 'subject to rough useage'.

Could this have held the desecrated remains of Mary's beloved father, rescued by her from a degrading fate and kept by her ever since?

The Vicar himself denied it, though it is said that he never actually saw into the vault himself. Perhaps he did not want the fuss and feared his church becoming a place of pilgrimage for ghoulish sensation-seekers or worse. Cromwell's biographers prefer to believe that the body was eventually reburied at Newburgh Priory, the Cromwell family home in the north where there is now a kiln-like brick tomb which has never since been opened.

If Mary did keep her father's body somewhere, it would have had a rather peripatetic existence for Mary and her husband did not come to live in Chiswick until fifteen years after it was first dug up. Where was it in the meantime?

Yet the legend lives on – never likely to be conclusively proved now as the Fauconberg vault lies buried under several inches of hard concrete under St Nicholas' church.

And what of the head, languishing so long on ignominious display at Westminster Hall?

The head, it seems, was blown down one night in 1685. A sentry hid it beneath his cloak and took it home. Over the next few centuries this grisly relic passed through the hands of many people, who treated it with varying degrees of respect. The sentry's family sold it to a family in Cambridgeshire; from 1710 to 1783 it was in a private museum in London; later in the 18th century it belonged to a poor actor at Covent Garden who kept it on show in Long Acre. In the 19th century it belonged to one Josiah Henry Wilkinson who used it as a visual aid while lecturing on phrenology. In the 20th century experts pronounced it genuine and it eventually was bequeathed to Cromwell's old college, Sidney Sussex, Cambridge, where it was finally given a decent burial in 1960.

The exact spot is, perhaps wisely, kept a well-guarded secret!

The Prophecies
of
Syon Abbey

❦

THE coffin stood on a table, dark shadows moving in the flickering candlelight. The gross bloated body of the King, the man who had once been a handsome prince sworn to defend the Catholic Church against the Protestant reformers, still seemed to sweat under its lid.

It was strange, the attendants thought as they left it for the night. It was strange and ironic that the body should rest here in Syon Abbey for it was this man, the late King Henry VIII, who had brought to an end its monastic status and taken the property to be his own in defiance of those brave souls who had warned that retribution, however long delayed, would follow.

There had been Elizabeth Barton, dubbed the 'Holy Maid of Kent', a poor servant girl afflicted with strange fits and visions, trances and prophesies. She had railed against the King's proposed second marriage, alleging that he would not survive for six months after putting away his rightful Queen, Catherine of Aragon. It was here in the cloisters at Syon that Sir Thomas More had conferred with her – at some risk to his own head as it turned out until he frankly and publicly admitted his error in listening to her. Elizabeth had not been pardoned though and had been executed at Tyburn in April 1534.

The King's Chief Minister Thomas Cromwell – partner in crime, some would say – had then sent his agent Thomas Layton to examine the state of affairs in the monastery, something that was happening up and down the country as King Henry tightened his grip on the English Church and its institutions. It was no surprise to the more cynical when Layton received a report 'certefyinge the Incontynnsye of the Nunnes of Syon with the Friores', falsely charging the peaceable inmates with all the sins he could think of, and the suppression of a community which dated back to 1415, and which had long enjoyed royal patronage, quickly followed.

In the following year, 1535, Brother Peto, a Franciscan friar, preached a strange and brave sermon with the King in attendance. Looking Henry firmly in the eye he declared that for what he was doing 'God's judgements were ready to fall upon his head' and that 'the dogs would lick his blood as they had done Ahab's', a divine judgement on the desecration of the monasteries.

And there would be many more martyrs. Father Richard Reynolds, a priest of Syon and a noted scholar of his day, refused to accept the King's supremacy over the Church. For this he was imprisoned and then executed at Tyburn – executed in the hideous manner of being hanged, drawn and quartered. Henry's ill-starred fifth wife, Catherine Howard, was confined at Syon – by now the King's property – from November

1541 until her execution in the following February.

Yes, they thought, it was ironic that now the King himself should lie unprotesting within the abbey walls.

The next morning a strange and awful sight awaited them. The King's bloated body had burst open during the night and round the coffin the dogs were licking up the offal.

And all remembered Brother Peto's prophecy.

The Lady of
Letters

T HE year is 1634. It is summer and on a fine evening
a Grand Masque is to take place in the grounds of
Harefield Place, sloping towards the little River Colne
on the far north-western fringe of the county.

The masque will be a fine occasion – magnificent
costumes designed by Inigo Jones, music by Henry
Lawes and words by Lawes' new friend, a serious-
minded young poet by the name of John Milton. It is
entitled *Grand Arcadia* and is intended as a humble
offering to a fine old lady, Alice, Countess of Derby,
whose life it is to celebrate.

And what a life it had been. Alice had been born into
one of England's most noble families. Her father was Sir
John Spencer of Althorp. Edmund Spenser, the poet,
wrote of her as did Milton and she probably saw
Shakespeare acting in a performance of *Othello*, staged at
Harefield in the presence of Queen Elizabeth herself!

Her first marriage was to the Earl of Derby and it was
during this time that Spenser dedicated to her his *Tears*

of the Muses, celebrating her as 'Sweet Amaryllis'. She clearly had an eye for a good marriage for when she was widowed she married the Lord Chancellor, Sir Thomas Egerton, in 1602. They purchased the mansion known as Harefield Place and prepared it for a visit from Gloriana herself, the aged Queen Elizabeth. In her last summer, Elizabeth spent three days from July 31st here in the depths of rural Middlesex and witnessed Shakespeare's company, the Lord Chamberlain's Players, act out the tragedy of the Moor of Venice – newly-written by their leading actor. The weather, we learn from verses presented to the Queen – not, it would seem from Shakespeare's pen – was poor:

> Only poor St Swithun now
> Doth hear you blame his cloudy brow.

The masque acted out how Elizabeth was met near the dairy house by a dairy-maid and a bailiff who celebrated her praises in alternate verses while the Queen sat on her horse, sheltering under a tree to keep out of the rain. As she was by then over seventy this indignity, if true, might have hastened her demise! The blandishments of such lines as

> Beauty's rose and virtue's book,
> Angel's mind and angel's look

may not have been quite enough to ease her impatience.

In the masque Alice was honoured as the Queen herself with such verses as

> Look, nymphs and shepherds, look,
> What sudden blaze of Majesty

31

Is that which we from hence descry?
Too divine to be mistook!
   This, this is she
To whom our vows and wishes bend;
Here our solemn search has end.

Mark what radiant state she spreads,
In circle round her shining throne,
Shooting her beams like silver threads;
   This, this she is alone,
Sitting like a goddess bright,
In the centre of her light.

Not Milton at the top of his form perhaps, but doubtless the elderly Alice, wrapped up against the cool of the evening, would have appreciated the compliment.

Alice too was now close to the end of her long and eventful life. In Harefield church, the home of many magnificent baroque memorials, hers is outstanding. She wears a rich red dress complete with collar and cuffs, a ruffled farthingale and an ermine cloak. She has fine beads round her neck and shoulders, and earrings and a coronet of gold. Her golden hair curls over her cushions and her hands are together in prayer. Coats of arms and Corinthian columns enrich the canopied monument which also bears images of her three daughters from her first marriage – like their mother they all did well in the matrimonial stakes, it would seem, for they all married earls! It is a fine memorial to a grand and formidable lady.

The landscape of Harefield is much changed from her day. The grand house was burned down in 1660, caused by the then owner, Sir Charles Sedley, profligate companion of Charles II, reading in bed and upsetting the candle. The park now contains the buildings of the famous Harefield Hospital. Yet the church remains, and the almshouses in the village, to recall earlier times.

King James
and
the Tinker

❧

CLOSE encounters with royalty are not what you might expect when you go out for a quiet drink nowadays. Things apparently were different in the 17th century if the story told at the King and Tinker pub on the edge of Enfield Chase is to be believed.

The nearby estate of Theobalds was one of King James I's favourite hunting grounds. There, as everywhere, he was feted by his courtiers and his every whim was catered for. But, perhaps like modern celebrities, he sometimes hankered after being just a normal person who could come and go as he pleased, unrecognised and unmolested.

One day while out riding with his nobles, James decided to do just that. He slipped away from his escort on Four Tree Hill and rode off into the woods. Deep in a secluded glade he came across an alehouse where a poor tinker sat drinking in the porch. A casual greeting, a comment on the weather and the sport and soon the two men were chatting like old friends.

'What news, honest fellow?' the King asked, posing as a stranger.

'I hear that good King James is out hunting the deer,' the old tinker replied. 'It would be grand to see him! Never in all my long days have I had such an honour.'

'Let's ride out and see if we can find him,' his new companion replied. 'Come up on my horse and we'll search.'

'We should know him by his fine clothes,' said the tinker as they made their way through the trees.

'And his nobles must surely be bareheaded in the royal presence,' James pointed out.

They reached Four Tree Hill again where the nobles were awaiting the King's return. They, of course, knew him well and at the sight of them doffed their hats and acknowledged their sovereign.

The poor tinker was mortified. What had he done? He had failed to do homage to the King! He had not bowed! He had not even removed his hat!

The tinker jumped from the King's horse and fell on his knees, pleading for mercy. Laughing, the King bade him rise. 'What is your name, good man?' he asked.

'John of the Vale,' the tinker replied, 'a mender of kettles and lover of good ale, if it please Your Majesty.'

'Then rise up, Sir John,' said the King, 'I will honour you here and create thee a knight of five hundred a year. Come, enjoy my hospitality.'

This tale is told in one of those old ballads that go on for verse after verse until the singer's audience is comatose with boredom. There are those academic spoilsports who will tell you that similar ballads are sung on the Scottish borders and that same story appears all over the place with different characters – King John and the miller of Charlton, Charles V of Spain and the cobbler of Brussels, even Haroun-al-Raschid, who used to go about his dominions incognito under the name of Il Bondocani.

But don't say such a thing in Enfield Chase if you know what's good for you!

The Silver Arrow

J OHN Lyon, a wealthy gentleman farmer of the hamlet of Preston within the parish of St Mary, Harrow-on-the-Hill, was a generous benefactor to education. Each year he set aside 'twenty marks' for the instruction of poor children and in 1571 he obtained letters patent and a charter from Elizabeth I, empowering him to found a 'Free Grammar School' at Harrow and to draw up statutes for its regulation and government.

From the most detailed instructions and provisions that he left in his will when he died in 1592, it is clear that he regarded archery as an essential part of the curriculum. To encourage this 'gentle art', he instituted a prize of a silver arrow to be shot for annually on the 4th of August, though this date was later changed to the first Thursday in July. Archery was seen as 'a worthy game, a wholesome kind of exercise and much commended in physic', as the eminent Bishop Latimer had described it in 1509.

At first there were six and later twelve competitors for John Lyon's silver arrow. The boy who first shot a dozen arrows closest to the bull's-eye was proclaimed the winner and carried off the prize, attended by a triumphal procession of his fellows.

The competitors were arrayed in fancy costumes of spangled satin in white and green, with sashes and silken caps. The Butts, beside the road from London, were at the edge of the village, backed by a lofty slope, cut back in terraces to make a natural amphitheatre.

In 1731 the winner was Master Brown, son of Captain Brown, commander of an East Indiaman; in 1757 Master Earle; in 1761 the Earl of Barrymore. In 1764 the winner was a Master Mee, whose grandson was another Harrovian, Lord Palmerston, the Victorian Prime Minister. In 1765 'some Indian warriors were present to witness the exhibition', according to a report in the *Gentleman's Magazine* for that year – but it does not state whether they were natives of the future Empire of India or Red Indians! One assumes the former.

In 1766 the silver arrow was won by Master Charles Wager Allix whose son, also called Charles, of Willoughby Hall, Lincolnshire wrote that 'several people remembered well my father's winning it and that it was warmly contested, one of the shooters being particularly desirous to gain it, inasmuch as three of his brothers in succession had previously been the victors. His father had stuck up three arrows already in three corners of his drawing room and so especially wanted the fourth to fill up the other corner.' This unnamed archer was to be unlucky, defeated by young Master Allix, and his disappointment comes right down the years to us. Perhaps the weight of family expectation was too much for him on the day.

This letter to a later headmaster recalls that Master Allix too had his problems. 'I have now the bow with which it was won,' his proud offspring recounted. 'My father has told me that only one week before the day of the shooting he discovered that it had been maliciously broken by someone. This discovery plunged him into the deepest despair; however he sent the bow immediately to London, for the chance of its being repaired. It was repaired but considerably shortened. Still to his inconceivable delight, he found upon trying it, that he could shoot with it better than ever and HE WON THE PRIZE.'

The arrow still forms part of the coat of arms of the school and Harrow is famous for the longevity of its traditions. Yet the Silver Arrow competition lapsed in the late 18th century. The last contest was in July 1771. In the September the headmaster, Dr Sumner, died and was succeeded by Dr Heath who did not wish the competition to continue.

He had his reasons. One of the competitors had recently caused a serious accident. It is alleged that he shot so far wide of the mark that his arrow struck a spectator in the eye, rather in the manner of King Harold at the Battle of Hastings. Another version of the tale says that the victim was a local barber named Godling and that he was, in fact, shot in the mouth. Whatever the true facts, it is clear that the incident brought a sudden end to the tradition – and not before time, perhaps!

There had been other problems as well – the competitors had come to regard it as a privilege not to be infringed upon that they should have frequent exemptions from lessons in order to practise and in recent years enjoyment of the event had been marred by the bands of unruly spectators which it brought to Harrow.

THE SILVER ARROW

The arrow made for the 1772 event was never shot for but remains in the school library. The woodland around The Butts was cleared in about 1810 and houses built on the site.

When the archery competitions were abolished public 'speeches' by senior boys were adopted in their place, held on the first Thursdays in May, June and July and a new Harrow School tradition became established.

The Man
who
Built a River

❧

You did not want to drink London's water in the time of Queen Elizabeth I. In those days the chief source of water was the River Thames – a dumping place for the city's rubbish and the contents of their chamber-pots and privies. Those folk unlucky – or perhaps lucky – enough not to live close to this foetid flow had to rely on springs and wells, which might be clear if you were fortunate, or on the door-to-door water carrier, a familiar sight with his yoke across his shoulders supporting two heavy barrels.

None of this was ideal in a crowded and growing city. Something had to be done. In 1570 an Act of Parliament authorised the construction of a 'river' – I suppose we might be more likely to call it a canal – to bring clean water from the heights of Middlesex to the north of the city and ambitious entrepreneurs and engineers began to fancy their chances.

Despite a false start or two, nothing much happened

until March 1609 when the Corporation of the City of London accepted an offer by a certain Hugh Myddelton to complete the work. Myddelton was a self-made man – he had had to be, being the sixth son of the governor of Denbigh Castle in North Wales. There cannot have been much of an inheritance left for a sixth son!

His enterprises back in North Wales had included a successful coal mine and by the time he was 40, in 1600, he had become an Alderman of the ancient borough of Denbigh and one of the Merchant Adventurers of England.

Like Isambard Kingdom Brunel in the Victorian era, Myddelton was ahead of his time and thought on a larger scale than most of his contemporaries. He envisaged a canal running from springs near Hertford all the way to Islington – a distance of ten miles as the crow flies but, as the canal had to run more or less level at about the 100 foot contour, the channel that needed to be cut was nearly 40 miles long, often passing along one side of a valley and back down the other. A major aqueduct, 600 feet long, was needed across the Salmon's Brook at Bush Hill near Enfield, carrying the New River in a massive lead-lined wooden trough, six feet wide and five feet deep.

Work started in April 1609 and on 29th September 1613 the sluicegates were opened and 'the sweet waters of Hertfordshire flowed into the Round Pond at Islington', at a site that is still known today as New River Head. The water was distributed around the city in pipes made from hollowed-out elm trunks. The end of each pipe was sharpened like a pencil and driven into the tapered bore of the next. Crude but effective for they did not start being replaced until the end of the 18th century.

Inevitably, not everyone had approved of the scheme. Like the Channel Tunnel or the Millennium Dome, the New River had faced opposition and ridicule, especially from the landowners across whose property it was to be built. There were serious financial problems and Myddelton had had to be supported by no less than King James I himself, who allowed the New River to be cut across the royal estates at Theobalds (near Enfield) free of charge. This was perhaps something of a surprise as the King, even in those malodorous times, was notoriously averse to water, both as a drink or as an aid to cleanliness!

The King may have regretted his generosity when on one occasion his horse stumbled while he was out riding and deposited him in the ice-covered water of the New River. He had to be rescued and taken back to Theobalds for a change of clothes and a warm bed!

The New River continues to wind its way across the Middlesex suburbs between Enfield and Islington. Within fifty years of its opening the flow from the Hertfordshire springs proved inadequate and it was decided to divert water from the River Lea – which was presumably cleaner then than it subsequently became. The owners of mills on the Lea protested vigorously since they depended on a full-flowing river and an Act of Parliament had to be introduced to monitor how much was being abstracted.

In 1780 a mob taking part in the disorder of the anti-Catholic Gordon Riots threatened to destroy the Bush Hill aqueduct, thus cutting off London's water supply, and a detachment of soldiers had to be billeted locally to protect it. In 1786, perhaps as a result of this threat, the aqueduct was taken down and replaced by a stretch of embankment.

Now the massive London Ring Main, another notable feat of engineering, constructed in the 1990s, supplies water from the reservoirs at Staines to be distributed around the metropolis via the water treatment works at Ashford Common and Hampton. With other reservoirs stretching down the Lea Valley and the impressive Victorian pumping engines at Kempton Park and Brentford now restored to working order, the landscape of Middlesex shows the imprint of the capital's insatiable thirst!

Stealing and Sorcery on Enfield Chase

❧

ENFIELD Chase is still largely open land, a survivor of the ancient Forest of Middlesex – home to deer and wild boar in medieval times and an area where the King's Forest Laws were jealously upheld. In those days, far from being a peaceful place, it was an area of much dispute and thievery, witnessed by surviving court records.

Many of these court records relate to cattle and pigs grazing on the common land being stolen off the Chase. In such cases Common Law rather than the Forest jurisdiction applied. In the 1270s, for example, a certain John Russell was arrested for stealing three pigs belonging to John Salmon and one belonging to John Mandeville of South Mymms. The jury, made up of tenants of the manors of Edmonton, Enfield and South Mymms, showed him no mercy. He was declared guilty and was hanged.

From the court archives it is very clear that the juries

were more ready to condemn strangers than local men when conviction carried the death penalty.

A series of bad harvests in the years following 1315 caused starvation and hardship resulting, unsurprisingly, in an increase in the number of thefts of food and animals from Enfield Chase. In the next four years there were 39 cases; 25 defendants were hanged and 12 acquitted. The remaining two were found guilty but being Clerks in Holy Orders – a somewhat elastic term in those days – successfully pleaded Benefit of Clergy and thereby saved their necks. Such was the endemic poverty of these poor unfortunates that of the 25 hanged, 18 were found to have no possessions at all and the rest were so poor that the combined value of all they owned was less than one pound.

It was not just the destitute who found themselves up before the court. In 1318 Thomas le Brewere, a respectable London tradesman, was arrested for being in possession of seven pigs belonging to Gilbert de Barnet and stolen off the Chase. It must have been a nightmare for this worthy citizen, doubtless aware of the fate of his predecessors in the dock, but he was able to prove to the jury's satisfaction that he had purchased the pigs from one Roger Pycard for 20 shillings in front of honest witnesses and neighbours in the Ward of Cripplegate in the City of London.

Now it was Pycard's turn to face the music. He denied that he was the one who had stolen the pigs but it seems that the evidence against him was too strong. He was found guilty and hanged. The court affirmed that le Brewere could not have known that the pigs were stolen when he bought them, paying a fair market price. Gilbert de Barnet found himself fined for making a false accusation against him. Le Brewere's name was cleared but sadly there is no record of his hard-earned 20 shillings being returned to him.

A pig also featured in a notorious 17th century court case which hinted at sinister Black Arts being practised on the fringes of the Chase. Elizabeth Sawyer, dubbed 'The Witch of Edmonton', lived in the remote woodland hamlet of Winchmore Hill which lay in Edmonton parish. A trivial quarrel with a neighbour escalated to the extent that the neighbour struck Elizabeth's prized pig. Mother Sawyer was then alleged to have threatened: 'that will be a dear blow to you.'

The neighbour promptly fell ill and died. There was no apparent reason for her demise and in those superstitious times any unpopular eccentric might find herself accused of witchcraft. It was a difficult allegation to refute in view of the evidence of the neighbour's death. The case went to the Old Bailey where Elizabeth was tried and convicted and she was hanged at Tyburn in 1621. These events became the subject of a famous play and prints were produced, showing Edmonton's 'Witch' as an evil, bent old woman, though she was in fact just 48 years old.

Even in more modern times the wildwoods and heaths of Enfield Chase have been avoided by the wary on dark lonely nights!

The Umbrella Man

MOURNERS standing at a graveside in Hanwell churchyard on a wet winter's morning might well have cause to be grateful to one Jonas Hanway of Red Lion Square who lies buried there, for Mr Hanway is credited with being the first man to use an umbrella in London. If though, after the funeral, they had been denied a reviving cup of tea, they might have been less keen to praise his name!

It must have been quite a brave thing to do in the mid 18th century: walking the streets under such a curious and outlandish contraption, ignoring the jeers of passers-by and the ribald shouts of the coachmen. 'It may be regarded as a trivial matter,' wrote Samuel Smiles in *Self Help*, 'but let any modern London merchant venture to walk along Cornhill in a peaked Chinese hat, and he will find it takes some moral courage to persevere in it.' The early bicyclists must have suffered much the same experience yet by the end of his life Jonas Hanway saw his novel practice widely adopted.

Not that he was fearful of causing controversy – a much travelled man in his younger days, he became an avid and controversial writer of earnest tracts on a variety of subjects, one of the best-known of his day. Perhaps, though, some of his contemporaries found him a bit of a bore!

Dr Johnson gives us the flavour of the man – 'he acquired some reputation by travelling abroad but lost it all by travelling at home,' he wrote – and Miss Burney described him as 'very loquacious, extremely fond of talking of what he has seen and heard, and would be very entertaining were he less addicted to retell anecdotes and reports from newspapers.' The original bar-room bore?

His father, who had been Agent Victualler for the Navy, was killed in an accident when his son was just a boy. Aged 17, Jonas was apprenticed to a Lisbon merchant in 1729. He did well and in 1743 a Mr Dingley, a merchant at St Petersburg, made him a partner. He became involved in the trade to Russia and Persia, his caravan of woollen goods en route from St Petersburg being plundered by rebels at Astrabad in 1744 and Hanway himself suffering what he described as 'many privations'.

A large inheritance in 1750 enabled him to retire from trade and devote himself to writing, beginning with an account of his travels in the East which was published in 1753. He then became a campaigner for all sorts of causes – a professional pundit, we might say today, although Carlyle described him as 'a dull, worthy man'.

Tea was one of his pet hates and he wrote the less than snappily-titled *Essay on Tea, considered as pernicious to Health, obstructing Industry, impoverishing the Nation etc.*, which had as much effect as King James I's ill-fated *Counterblast* against tobacco. He became involved in all sorts of philanthropic schemes such as the founding of the Marine Society in 1756 for the purpose of keeping up a supply of sailors for the Navy.

A portrait of Hanway in the offices of the Marine Society in Bishopsgate shows him seated at a table, dressed in a fashionable blue suit of the period, complete with ruffles, and a face strongly marked with benevolence and good sense.

He was concerned about the state of London's roads and the high infant mortality among the poor. He visited some of the city's worst slums in his campaigning and petitioned for the protection of the youngsters who were sent up the capital's sooty chimneys as sweeps, which resulted in an Act of Parliament being passed for their protection. The provision of Sunday schools was another of his 'good causes' as was, from another of his verbose titles, *The Great Advantage of Eating Pure and Genuine Bread, comprehending the Heart of the Wheat with all its flour.*

Perhaps it is no surprise that such an opinionated man never married. Like other philanthropists and supporters of worthy endeavours, Jonas Hanway sometimes allowed his passion for causes to get in the way of his common sense. His first book, the one on his epic travels, was surely his most interesting. On a more local level, he also published an account of the journey from Kingston to Portsmouth!

After that, perhaps you could easily have too much of this 'Man of Opinions', but he is, for all that, one of the more interesting worthies to be buried in Middlesex.

Bent Bonds!

❧

COWLEY is now an anonymous suburban district between Uxbridge and West Drayton but was, in times long gone, a pleasant scattered village along the Frays Stream, a tributary of the Colne. In the churchyard, close to the tower, lies the unmarked grave of the Reverend Doctor William Dodd, an eloquent preacher and King's chaplain whose spectacular fall from grace ended with his being hanged for forgery in 1777.

To be appointed one of the King's chaplains was a great honour though the duties, attending the Court and taking occasional services in the royal household, may not have been onerous. William Dodd was one of the 'bright young things' of the day. The son of the Vicar of Bourne in Lincolnshire, he had a good education and privileged status – but like many born with the proverbial 'silver spoon' in his mouth, he went off the rails in a big way. A wild youth and a marriage to a disreputable woman foreshadowed his sad end.

At first all went well. Before being ordained, he wrote a novel and compiled a hugely popular book, *The Beauties of Shakespeare*, which included all the best-loved extracts. He became tutor to the Earl of Chesterfield and had an enviable reputation for his sermons and commentaries on the Bible. Today he would doubtless have been a media celebrity appearing on chat-shows and in the gossip columns. He was even a lottery-winner which rather went to his head and encouraged him to seek the prestigious position of Rector of St George's, Hanover Square, one of the most fashionable and exclusive congregations in the capital.

But behind the glitzy façade Dodd must have lacked confidence, or perhaps despite his lottery success he lacked the financial resources to sustain his high social standing. Whatever the reason, it was discovered that, in order to obtain the position at St George's, he had bribed the Lord Chancellor's wife. He was ruined financially and disgraced.

To get out of the mess he found himself in, Dodd forged the signature of his former pupil, the Earl of Chesterfield, on a bond or promissory note for £4,200 – a large enough sum even these days, let alone in the 18th century. He almost got away with it. The note was deposited with a solicitor for safe custody. The solicitor noticed a blot on one of the letters of the signature and, being a cautious man, thought it advisable to get a fresh signature. When approached to do this, the Earl of course immediately denounced the note as a forgery and the Reverend Doctor was in deep trouble.

He fled but was discovered hiding in an old farmhouse in the parish of Whitton, close to Hounslow Heath, and was arrested. He actually had the funds to pay back most of the money at once and promised to raise the balance as soon as he could. But forgery was just one of many capital offences in those days – the government taking all measures possible to protect the reputation of the currency against fraud and speculation – and the authorities determined to prosecute their high-profile victim as a public example. He was found guilty and sentenced to death.

They had reckoned without public opinion. Dodd was a popular man. The eminent Doctor Johnson took pity on him and wrote him a speech to be used in a plea for mitigation of his sentence. When that failed, he wrote him a 'Convict's Address to his Unhappy Bretheren'. Both of these the irrepressible Dodd delivered as his own work. Some people never learn!

Some 77,000 people signed a petition for clemency. The Lord Mayor of London called on King George III to grant a reprieve to his former chaplain, but to no avail. In his last days Dodd's many friends subscribed £1,000 with which to bribe the jailer into letting him escape! There were reports that on the night before his execution a man was seen lurking around Newgate Jail with the money in his hand, hoping for a last-minute change of heart.

But Dodd was indeed hanged and his body taken through the Middlesex lanes to remote little Cowley, to the church where his older brother Richard was Rector.

Yet was that unmarked grave in Cowley churchyard really William Dodd's last resting place? For years afterwards there was a persistent tradition that a certain Doctor Hunter had quickly cut him down from the gallows, taken him to a coffee house, revived him by submerging him in hot water and smuggled him over to France where he was later seen alive and well. Was William Dodd in that long tradition of well-connected criminals who escaped justice to live out their days comfortably abroad?

His brother Richard said nothing more of the matter but, in memory of his brother, he left the sum of £100 in his will of 1811, to be invested by the churchwardens in consolidated bank annuities, the interest to be distributed annually to the poor of Cowley.

Such ancient bequests are all submerged in the wider finances of the Church of England today and the story of William Dodd has been all but forgotten in the parish in which he might – or might not – lie buried.

The Foiling
of King John

❧

THE little market town of Staines was shaken out of its usual placid existence by the arrival of King John and his retinue. The streets thronged with soldiers and the sounds of horsemen. The young women of the town had high hopes, some of them, of what the next few nights might bring – a change from dull routine certainly, if nothing better. The taverns were full and the strange folk from up London were watched cautiously by the men of Middlesex.

The next day the procession headed west out of the town, across Staines Bridge, then the only one to cross the Thames above London and Kingston. Indeed the bridge was one of the reasons for the choice of the procession's final destination: it enabled England's barons to come with their liegemen conveniently from all corners of the realm. For they were headed a little further yet: westward, following the river to fair Runnymede. The year was 1215 and the name on everyone's lips was 'Magna Carta'. Staines and its bridge, besides taking travellers westward on many lawful and uneventful occasions, were playing

their part in the history of England!

Grimly the barons had the previous day ridden across the featureless tracks of Hounslow Heath, past the one-street straggling township of Hounslow itself, past the newly-built priory of the Holy Trinity and out across the flat plains. This time they meant business.

King John had shown himself to be a dictator, a despotic tyrant who flouted the rights of his subjects. With the support of the Church, in the person of Archbishop Langton of Canterbury, they knew that for once they were stronger than the King and were determined to settle their just grievances on their own terms.

The King submitted at Runnymede. Indeed he had no choice, but his word meant nothing to him. He was just playing for time while his agents recruited enough mercenary soldiers abroad to enable him to crush his opponents. He returned to Windsor Castle to make his plans.

But the barons had their spies out and word got back to their leader, Robert Fitz-Walter. He was told that the King was scheming to seize London and the Tower as soon as they had dispersed to a planned tournament in Stamford. Calling for his scribe and messengers, Fitz-Walter dictated his response:

Robert Fitz-Walter, Marshal of the Army of God and the Holy Church and other nobles of the same army send greeting.

You well know of how great importance it is to you and to us all to keep possession of the City of London, which is a place of refuge to us, and what a disgrace it would be if through any fault of ours we were to lose it.

Be it known to you as a fact that we have been forewarned that there are some who are only waiting for our departure from the aforesaid city to take possession of it on a sudden.

Therefore, by the general advice of all we have put off the tournament which was to commence at Stamford on the Monday next after the Feast of the Apostles Peter and Paul.

But there will be a tournament near London, in the Staines Wood and at the town of Hounslow. This we have done for our safety and the safety of the aforesaid city. And we therefore enjoin and earnestly beseech you to come to the tournament aforesaid, well-provided with horses and arms that you may there obtain honour.

Whoever performs well there will receive a bear which a lady will send to the tournament.

Farewell.

Stirring words indeed and a source of anger and frustration to the wicked King back at Windsor.

Somewhere on the heaths and commons between Staines and Hounslow the tournament was held. We don't know exactly where. Ashford, Bedfont, Feltham, Hanworth – all are possibilities and all somewhat unlikely settings for noblemen to disport themselves nowadays. It takes quite an effort of the imagination to picture joustings, archery competitions, tumblers, acrobats and all the accoutrements of a medieval tournament in the environs of Heathrow Airport!

But if it hadn't happened our national history and our precious traditional liberties could have been very different.

The Chain Gang
on
Hounslow Heath

❧

IT must have been an odd sight – the watching villagers of Hampton and Hanworth had never seen the like. A couple of toffs prancing around on the heath with long chains and glass rods, noting strange figures down in their notebooks and the whole time being guarded and assisted by a detachment of soldiers. What was the world coming to?

'It'll cost us money, I'll be bound,' the habitual pessimist opined.

The year was 1783, the place Hounslow Heath and the strange activity was the culmination of nearly forty years of frustration and effort.

Back in 1745 the Jacobite Rebellion had come as something of a shock to the military planners of the day. More than once the pride of Britain's army had got embarrassingly lost in the mists and glens of the Scottish Highlands. The government had become convinced of the need for a careful survey of the country in order to produce accurate large-scale maps to prevent such a thing happening again.

Things moved slowly – the Seven Years War caused a delay that was considerably longer and it was not until 1783, twenty years after the peace treaty that ended that particular conflict, that the two men entrusted with supervising this task were able to start work. Major General William Roy was a career soldier and he was assisted in the survey task by the President of the Royal Society, Sir Joseph Banks of Spring Grove, Isleworth.

The key word was 'Triangulation'. This depended on the geometrical principle that if you measured a baseline accurately on the ground, and then made this line one side of a triangle whose third point was a distant but highly visible feature, you could then calculate – not having to measure – the length of the other two sides by observing the angles they made with the third side using elementary trigonometry. Once that was done, the process could be repeated using other prominent features of the landscape, building up yet more triangles until the whole country had been covered. Who says those geometry lessons at school were a waste of time?

Roy and Banks had had a trial run earlier in the year, measuring across the fields between Marylebone and St Pancras but, perhaps because of the local knowledge provided by Sir Joseph, decided that Hounslow Heath would be the ideal location on which to establish the initial baseline. Roy praised its 'great extent and the extraordinary levelness of its surface without any local obstruction whatever to render measurements difficult'.

They had to clear the straight line thus measured, removing bushes and undergrowth, making a path three or four yards wide. A sergeant, corporal and ten men of the 12th Regiment of Foot were brought from

Windsor to assist and set up camp at the edge of
Hanworth Park. The soldiers were preferred, being
'more attentive to orders than country labourers'. The
first instrument used was an ordinary hand-held
telescope, but Roy soon realised the need to have this
fixed to a tripod. A high steeple over ten miles away
proved to be a suitable sighting point.

The baseline was measured in three sections: Hampton
Poor House to Hanworth Park; Hanworth Park to the
Staines road; the Staines road to King's Arbour, a point on
the edge of the heath between Cranford Bridge and
Longford. In order to mark the two end points, iron
pillars six feet long and one foot in diameter were
rammed into the ground. At the top of each was a bore
four inches in diameter and two feet deep. These are still
spoken of locally as guns or cannons to this day.

Roy used steel chains for the first measurements but
found that these were affected by the temperature.
Wooden rods were then experimented with. They had
to be free from knotholes and straight-grained so that if
they got wet they swelled across the grain and not along
it. Lengths of between twenty-five and thirty feet would
be needed. Banks' contacts resulted in suitable old masts
being supplied from the naval yards at Deptford. The
rods were not put end to end but slightly overlapping,
lining up marks made on them. The idea was that then
any errors made would cancel each other out.

However, even then the degree of accuracy was not
good enough – changing humidity still led to distortions
– and they next tried glass rods. These were specially
manufactured by Jesse Ramsden, the leading instrument
maker at the time. They were housed in wooden boxes
from which the ends stuck out. The tubes were supported at each end and at three evenly-spaced points

along their length. Lining-up markers were provided and thermometers inside the box made it possible to allow for any expansion and contraction of the glass due to changes in temperature.

Science was the great hope of the age and the work on Hounslow Heath attracted the attention of the great and the good. The wealthy Joseph Banks had marquees put up near to the site and there he entertained distinguished guests in some style. King George III himself gave great support and offered to pay for the manufacture by Ramsden of a fine theodolite for precision measurement of the triangles that were to be laid out.

Sadly it was this theodolite that hastened General Roy's death in 1790. Roy became increasingly frustrated at the delay in making this vital piece of technology. Ramsden was a perfectionist and could not be hurried. Roy had waited decades to get on with his pet project and was an old man in a hurry. He died suddenly while working on the proofs of his published report to the Royal Society. The language he had used against poor Ramsden in this report was apparently 'so violent that it had to be excised'!

However, General Roy's work is his memorial. In 1791, the year after his death, King George III established Britain's national survey which continues to produce definitive maps to this day. The same year the original measured baseline, five miles long, was checked with the very latest equipment and found to be only two and three-quarter inches out.

Hardy walkers using their Ordnance Survey maps as a lifeline in blizzard conditions in upland areas far more rugged than Hounslow Heath have good cause to be thankful to Major General William Roy – but perhaps they owe a debt to Bonnie Prince Charlie as well!

Romance
and Oliver Cromwell's
Daughter

❦

FRANCES Cromwell, youngest daughter of Oliver Cromwell, is buried in St Nicholas' church at Chiswick. She is little remembered now but had there been tabloid newspapers in her day, the trials, complexities and tragedies of her personal life would have kept her in the headlines.

At the time when the Puritan excesses of Cromwell's Protectorate had made ordinary folk long for the 'good old days' of Charles I, some of his advisors recommended that Frances should be married off to the young Prince Charles in order to restore peace and the monarchy. The Earl of Orrery was dispatched to put this proposal before the Lord Protector. It must have been a delicate task but the deed was done, even to the extent of petitioning Oliver's wife to support the match. No one seems to have consulted the young lady herself but it did not matter in the end for Cromwell is believed to have replied, 'Charles will never forgive me for the death of his father,' before adding, 'besides he is so debauched that he cannot be trusted.'

News of the failure of this plan cannot have come as bad news to Jeremiah White, Cromwell's chaplain, who was himself smitten by Frances' charms. She was quite keen on him too but both feared what her father's reaction to such a union might be. Matters came to a head when he caught them together in Frances' room!

The nervous young minister rose from his knees and let go of Frances' hand which he had been kissing. He knew he was in trouble.

'What is the meaning of this posture before my daughter?' Cromwell roared, although he had already been warned by his spies about the liaison.

White thought quickly, concerned that he should not lose his head (literally!). Pointing to Frances' maidservant who was standing nearby he improvised an excuse: 'May it please your lordship, I have a long time courted that gentlewoman there and cannot prevail. I therefore prayed upon her ladyship to intercede for me.'

It was a good story on the spur of the moment but young Jeremiah had not thought it through. It gave the Lord Protector an ideal chance to rid himself of a potential son-in-law who did not match up to his ambitions for his daughter. 'What is the meaning of this?' he expostulated to the frightened young woman. 'He is my friend and I expect you to treat him as such.'

Now this young servant clearly had an eye to the main chance. For her the young man represented a once-in-a-lifetime chance for a rise in status. To be a clergy wife offered her escape from a life of drudgery. 'If Mr White intends me that honour I shall not oppose him,' she replied demurely, casting a satisfied glance at her trapped and accidental suitor.

Oliver sent for another priest and had them married forthwith, giving the bride the fine sum of £500. Whether this gift was enough to resign Jeremiah to his fate it is impossible to know but it seems that they remained married for fifty years. Did they ever look back with amusement and affection, perhaps, to the strange circumstances that brought them together?

What poor Frances thought of this turn of events it is impossible to say but the complex tale of her on-off liaisons was not at an end A new suitor came onto the scene: Robert Rich, grandson and heir to the Earl of Warwick. He was deemed much more suitable and a magnificent and imposing wedding took place on 11th November 1657. All seemed set fair for Frances at last but within nine weeks her husband had been taken ill and had died, leaving her as a young widow.

Another member of the aristocracy, Sir John Russell, then sought her hand in marriage and duly wed her but he too died not long afterwards, leaving her a widow for the second time. She must have thought herself ill-starred. Did the idea cross her mind that all this might be a divine punishment for being the daughter of a regicide?

Fifty years a widow, the last relic of the tempestuous days of the Civil War when her family brought the monarchy to an end, albeit temporary, Frances Cromwell died on 27th January 1720 – in a very different age – after surviving all her brothers and sisters.

Unmasking
the Plot

~~~

'Train up a child in the way he should go, and when he
is old he will not depart from it'

THIS worthy inscription is to be found on the
Jacobean schoolhouse at Stanwell, an unlikely
survival – albeit now in a different use – to find so close
to the runways of Heathrow Airport. Yet the building
stands, much as when it was first built, endowed by the
bequest of the first and only Baron Knyvett of Stanwell
Place.

The Lord of the Manor of Stanwell, Baron Knyvett
also held the post of Sheriff of Westminster and it was in
this capacity that he received the warning that led him,
with a party of soldiers, to search the cellars below the
Palace of Westminster on the night of 4th November
1605 and to the discovery of Guy Fawkes and the
Gunpowder Plot.

A letter had been sent by some of the conspirators to
an ally, the Catholic Lord Monteagle, warning him not
to attend Parliament on November 5th: 'I would advise

you as you tender your life to devise some excuse to shift your attendance at this Parliament; for God and man hath concurred to punish the wickedness of this time. And think not slightly of this advertisement but retire yourself into the country where you may expect the event in safety, for though there be no appearance of any stir, yet I say they shall receive a terrible blow this Parliament and they shall not see who hurts them.'

Monteagle was not quite the friend that the plotters expected for he handed the letter over to the authorities.

It is clear that James I's ministers, led by Robert Cecil, now Earl of Salisbury, had no idea who the threat came from. They did not know their names, nor their whereabouts. No attempt was made to arrest the conspirators, who stayed safely in London until the plot was discovered and thwarted, then fled unmolested into the country. Had they not then betrayed themselves by attempting to start a revolt, all of them would have escaped – except for their unfortunate and devoted fall guy, Fawkes, who spent the nervous hours lurking in the cellars, pretending to be a watchman.

At three in the afternoon of the 4th, the Earl of Suffolk casually challenged this watchman. He had noticed the pile of kindling and faggots an the floor. 'Who do these belong to?' he enquired. Despite his awareness of the risks, indeed the probability that the plot was discovered, Guy Fawkes amazingly tried to bluff his way out of the difficulty.

'Percy,' he replied naming someone on whom there could be no suspicion.

He seemed to have got away with it as the Earl left him.

At ten o'clock one of his fellow conspirators slipped in to wish him Godspeed and to leave him a timepiece to mark the slow passing of time before he should light the fuse.

At ten minutes to midnight Knyvett came with his men and the game was up. Guy Fawkes was set upon and bound with his own garters. He was dragged to the Tower of London where, over the next few days, repeated torture gradually persuaded him to reveal the full details. He was executed on 1st February 1606.

Even now the fears of further Catholic plots made the King and his supporters wary. London was deemed to be unsafe for the upbringing of Prince Charles' three year old daughter, the Princess Mary. Nor was the sickly child's health too good and it was decided to send her away to live in Knyvett's rural household in Stanwell – 'to breathe the sweet air of Middlesex', as the King himself put it. What would that lover of pure air and hater of the habit of smoking tobacco say of the kerosine-polluted, fume-laden atmosphere of modern Stanwell, I wonder?

It was to no avail. The young girl died at Stanwell in 1607 and it must have been a great grief to the Baron, for he had no children of his own. Her body was brought back from Stanwell – a sorry little convoy that must have been – and buried in Westminster Abbey with her sister, Sophie. The place is still known as Innocents' Corner.

Lord and Lady Knyvett died childless in 1622, leaving provision for the building and endowment of a free school in the village. It may be that they saw this as a tribute and memorial to little Mary.

Their own memorial is in Stanwell's fine church – a marble monument carved by Nicholas Stone, much of whose work is in Westminster Abbey itself. Both have rich robes and fine Tudor ruffs of a bygone age even then. The desk at which they kneel is adorned with cherubs.

Lord Knyvett, devoted servant of the Stuart family, would have been pained had he known that in the next generation Stanwell would become Puritan and Parliamentary in sympathy during the Civil War – so strongly opposed to the Royalist cause that the villagers turned out their Vicar, Bruno Ryves, because he was Charles I's personal chaplain. They threw his possessions into a ditch and caused him to flee to Windsor for shelter.

How different history might have been had Lord Knyvett not carried out that midnight search!

Surviving
the
Black Hole

❧

THE old man woke suddenly, shaking and crying out
in his bedroom at Pinner Place. Eyes staring
sightless in the darkness, that old feeling of asphyxia
holding down his chest. Another nightmare.

Alerted by the commotion his night nurse, who had
been reading by the fire in the dressing-room, came in
to hold him briefly, to reassure him, to smooth down his
pillow, rearrange the sheets and see that all was well.

He recognised her, smiled weakly and was calm
again.

She looked down at him sadly. Another nightmare,
the third this week. Even in his old age he would never
be free of them.

It was the year of Our Lord 1798 and John Zephaniah
Holwell was dying. The son of a timber merchant, he
had been well educated and trained as a surgeon at
Guy's Hospital. In 1732, when he was 21 years old, he

sailed to Calcutta as a surgeon's mate in an Indiaman and settled there.

Young and ambitious he gave up surgery and, seeing that there was more money in it, he took up the remunerative administrative post of Zemindar, collecting tax revenues and acting as district governor. He was well suited to the post, having a flair for languages and an interest in the study of Hindu antiquities.

The East India Company was concerned with trade not political or military control, but trade often brings conflict. Local merchants resented British intrusion and local rulers, such as Siraj-ud-Daulah, Nawab of Bengal, felt threatened. Mercenary soldiers were used to protect the trading bases and keep the natives in line.

In June 1756 the Nawab, angry that the British had constructed fortifications against his wishes, attacked Calcutta. The Governor, not showing conspicuous bravery it would seem, abandoned the fort and retreated with most of his officers to a naval ship anchored offshore. Two hundred defenders were left and, as the most experienced man present, Holwell was appointed commander. In truth he had very little left to command! Bravely he led the defence until the ammunition ran out and they were forced to surrender.

Tense negotiations followed. Despite all that had happened Holwell believed that he was dealing with an honourable victor and had faith in the Nawab's promise that they would be well treated. At first they were, but towards evening some of the Company's mercenary soldiers got drunk and assaulted some natives. The Nawab then ordered that the British be treated as prisoners and put under guard.

All 146 of them, both men and women, were herded together in a small guardroom, 18 feet by 15 feet, with one door and two small barred windows. There was no food or water. The date was 20th June 1756, a hot humid evening, waiting for the monsoon to break.

Distress and panic set in quickly. The prisoners sweated profusely in such a confined and crowded place. The air was foul and they began to vomit all over each other. There was no room to breathe and they were tormented by thirst and breathlessness. They cried out for water and struggled frantically with each other when the Indian guards brought two hatfuls of water to the windows. Each individual was intent on their own needs. What remained of the water was spilled before the people on the far side of the room could get any. There was little Christian compassion or charity. Some prayed to their Creator, it is true, but many others blasphemed Him.

They remembered how they had looked up to John Zephaniah Holwell, however. He had won their respect, both as a just ruler and administrator for the East India Company in happier times and by his bravery in the past few days. They were brave too, those ordinary folk who were now dying slowly in the foetid darkness. They held their leader in such honour that some sacrificed themselves, insisting that he be placed close to the only window so that, with the help of what little fresh air there was, he might yet survive.

He sustained himself as best he could, slaking his thirst by wringing sweat from his drenched shirt and drinking it. He appealed for people to keep calm and tried unsuccessfully to bribe the guards, offering them 2,000 rupees to at least divide the prisoners into two groups and hold some elsewhere. As the night wore on, his discomfort lessened but only because, bemused and stupified, he began to lose his grip on reality.

Yet survive he did, survive that pit of cruelty that we still remember as The Black Hole of Calcutta, though the phrase is often used as a joke in these unfeeling times. In the morning there were only 23 left alive.

He was though a broken and exhausted man. Barely aware of what was happening, he was taken out and led into the presence of his captor, Siraj-ud-Daulah, the Nawab of Bengal himself. Yet now there came a miracle – his reputation as a fair and just man came to his rescue. His saviour was the Nawab's own grandmother, a strong woman whose words had always carried weight. She reminded her grandson of Holwell's reputation for justice and mercy when he had had the power. Surely he deserved the same now?

He was released, unlike another survivor, Mary Carey, the teenage wife of a river pilot. She had lost her husband, mother and sister in the Black Hole. Yet her tender beauty had somehow survived the night and so impressed Siraj-ud-Daulah that he had her taken to his harem from which she was only freed some years later.

Siraj himself came to a bad end. In early 1757, Robert Clive recaptured Calcutta for the East India Company. A few months later, betrayed and deserted by his army, the Nawab was defeated by the British at the Battle of Plassey and his body was later found in a ditch.

John Zephaniah Holwell was appointed Governor of Bengal after Clive left. One of his first acts was to set up a monument in memory of the victims of the Black Hole, erected over the common grave in which the bodies had been laid. He later returned to England and devoted himself to literary pursuits.

Holwell's was the only account of what happened in that hot night in Calcutta in 1756. For a century or more it was used as an example of 'the uncivilized behaviour of native Indians' and to justify British imperialism. 'The heathen must have Christianity and democracy,' it was said. 'Remember the Black Hole!' More recent historians, both British and Indian, have queried some details – it is now believed that the number incarcerated was nearer 60. Holwell may have wanted to show himself in a good light to further his own career and the authorities may have had a vested interest in letting the exaggerations stand.

But whatever the exact numbers involved, it is clear that the memory of that awful night could never leave him. Even in his old age in Pinner – he was 87 when he died – the images haunted him still.

The Tragic Story
of Charles and
Mary Lamb

❧

IT felt good to be retiring. Thirty-three years as a clerk at the City office of the East India Company was long enough for anybody, in all conscience, especially for a man who relished being out in the open air, going for long walks with Mary, if she was well enough.

Mary! Mary! Beloved sister, yet his secret sorrow, Charles Lamb reflected as he shut his desk for the last time. What was to become of her?

Now was the time for looking back. A sad childhood it had been, really. A prestigious address to be born, it was true – Crown Office Row in the Temple – but father had been a mere barrister's clerk and there was very little money. Father ailing and failing and mother an invalid, having to work at home as a dressmaker and with a streak of madness that was her tragic gift to Mary. Mary, who had had to be mother to them all and was broken by it.

He remembered his own six week sojourn in the

madhouse at Hoxton when he was just 21.

And then, that awful day, when Mary in a fit of frenzy had killed her mother.

She could not be left, of course. She was consigned to proper care and Charles had had to abandon his hopes of a literary career, hopes inspired by the example of his schoolfriend Samuel Taylor Coleridge. His own stammer, that impediment that would never go away, had already put paid to any hopes of university and the Church. Now hopes of marriage were gone too. Once his father had died in 1799 and he had made a home for poor Mary, and became legally her guardian. He could no longer hope or expect that dear Ann, his true love, could share his life.

So South Sea House and then East India House it had been. Walking out with Mary when she was well, and if she was not, going with her and then leaving her to be cared for at the asylum.

In the empty house of an evening he had written and written and written some more – anything really, just to increase his earnings a little. Verse, sonnets on his lost love (how poignant they were to write!), little paragraphs for the newspapers – even drama, although that had been a disaster, never to be attempted again.

But there had been the successes, he thought, smiling as he walked down the familiar stairs for the last time. *Tales from Shakespeare* which he had written with Mary for the children that they would never have, *Essays of Elia* appearing monthly in the *London Magazine* – wit, wisdom and humour that he had somehow been able to find within himself and bring out into the sunshine and add to it. Black humour too, drawn out of the insanity which he had learned to live with and control, painfully doing for himself what he could not do for Mary.

They could not stay long in any one place, that was the trouble. Each time Mary's problem became known about – and the attacks were becoming more and more frequent and severe – the neighbours would make it clear that they were no longer welcome. How often had they moved now? Five, six times? 'To change habitations', he thought, 'is to die in them and in my time I have died many deaths.'

He remembered Enfield: the two years in that delightful house in Gentlemen's Row and the walks, the green fields and lanes of the Chase. Heaven just at the end of the road and the rent £10 a year, less than at Islington. Then the two houses on Chase Side, first The Poplars with its pillared portico and then the move next door – '42 inches nearer Town,' he had joked – to Westwood Cottage, so that Mrs Westwood could better care for Mary.

He was walking along the street now and recalling Thomas Westwood, the schoolboy he had given the run of his library. How he wished he had a son of his own to do this for! When they had had literary visitors at The Poplars, what a pleasure it was to knock on the Westwoods' window and invite Tom to come in and meet his friends, Hazlitt, Tom Hood, Leigh Hunt, Coleridge, Wordsworth – they had all been there and he knew the boy had the wit to appreciate their conversation.

And the old cobbler, remember him? Stitching and repairing the backs of his books as the boy watched spellbound.

Now it was to be Edmonton: Bay Cottage, fitted in between two bigger houses, set back from the street and with a long narrow garden. They were to lodge with Mr and Mrs Walden as they had done with the Westwoods and Mary would be fine this time, surely.

But Charles Lamb was not to find any happiness at Edmonton. Mary was no better and when the madness took her had to be confined in a cupboard for her own safety. His lifelong friend Coleridge died – 'I feel how great a part he was of me,' Charles wrote. 'His great and dear spirit haunts me.'

His own death came mercifully quickly, a year and a half after the move to Edmonton. A stumble in the street, a head cut when he fell against a stone, going home cheerfully enough and laughing it off, but then within days fever and delirium.

Mary did not know what had happened and seemed not to react at all.

But how often in the thirteen years of twilight that were left to her did she cry out for the hand of the gentle brother who had guided her?

The Battle
of
Turnham Green

❧

THE morning after the battle they came out cautiously to number the dead. Crop-headed Parliamentary troops, some veterans from Edgehill where it all began, some from the Trained Bands of London, and some young apprentices who had never before seen an enemy. Eight hundred Royalists dead, someone said afterwards, though that might have been bravado and exaggeration in a just cause.

It was clear though that the King had lost many of the better sort. Gentlemen, judging by their apparel, for the Royalist losses were mainly among the mounted horsemen rather than the foot soldiers who had hung back from the fray. Four guns on their ungainly wheels had been abandoned too and fell into the hands of the rebels. On their own side they counted barely a hundred dead and gave them burial as best they could.

They fully expected a further fight. During the night the Royalists had more than once caused alarm by a quick incursion and the Roundheads had been ready to welcome them with fire and bullets as before. But each time they had fallen back and much of the night had passed quietly – or as quiet as it could given the drinking, damning and roaring coming up from the Royalist camp as the cavalry blamed the foot soldiers for their reverse, calling them cowards for not advancing, and the bloody infantrymen swore back at them.

If the King had expected to deal with London as easily as his forces had routed the isolated Parliamentarian regiments at Brentford the day before – a vicious little skirmish followed by a satisfying plundering of the town – he was to be disappointed. All through that evening, 11th November 1642, trained bands and volunteers from the City had been hastening along the road out of London towards the west. On the morning of the 12th, he had found his way barred by an army of some 24,000 men drawn up on the common at Turnham Green. The Royalists were outnumbered by about two to one.

Sheltering behind hedges and ditches the King's enemies were well placed to stop his advance, and determined to protect London from pillage or fire. Prince Rupert, the King's commander, had no desire to confront them directly and spread his lines out cautiously.

But Parliament's men, having in view those deadly enemies to God and their country, would not wait any longer and gallantly gave charge, the ordnance thundering their dreadful shot upon them with good aim, bringing down many of the horsemen. The Prince, desperate as well as valiant, laid about him in a fury and was marvellously unharmed by the firing all around him.

Yet they had to withdraw and so quietly did they do so

as the dusk fell, with no shout of command or beat of drum, that their foes were taken unawares at first, but then followed until it was too dark to see them.

'Aye, we'll give them a breakfast of the same viands that they've feasted on at supper!' prophesied one voice in the Parliament's camp after their prayers to mark a glorious victory, promising more of the same on the morrow.

But he and his comrades in arms were to be denied. The Prince was given a rousing 'Good Morning' with gunfire when he led a scouting party out first thing but thereafter he had no taste for a second drubbing and kept his troops well back out of musket range. The hedges and bushes that had given the rebels welcome protection the day before now looked likely to hinder them in any advance towards the King's lines.

Stalemate.

A vigorous Royalist attack round the north flank might have settled the issue in their favour but perhaps the Royalists now feared the threat from a force under Sir John Ramsay, holding the bridge at Kingston on behalf of Parliament. In fact this force had instead been ordered to fall back defensively towards the capital but, in the event, the Royalists retreated to occupy Kingston themselves, before finally withdrawing to Reading and Oxford.

A turning-point in the war – 12th November 1642. The King never again came as close to winning London.

Dreaming
of a
Lord Mayor

⁓∾

Sᴵʀ William Staines had done well in life and prospered. He was proud of his humble origins – just to make things complicated, he did not come from Staines at all but from Uxbridge where he started his working life as a bricklayer's labourer and at City banquets in later life he would tell a curious tale of a premonition.

One of his first jobs was on repairs to the parsonage house in his home town. As he was climbing up a ladder one day with his hod of mortar, the Vicar's wife called out to him and said that she had had a most extraordinary dream.

She told the astonished young man – who she had not known at all before – that she had dreamed that one day he would be Lord Mayor of London!

Young William did not know what to make of this but did not take it seriously. 'Strange woman!' he must have thought, perhaps a little embarrassed that he should figure so prominently in the night-time thoughts of a clergyman's wife.

'I have neither money nor influential friends,' he told her, laughing it off.

But the dream was repeated a second night and again the lady told William all about it.

He did well in business and in the affairs of the county and was eventually appointed Sheriff. He remembered the dream of the parson's wife and invited her husband, by then an elderly man, to be his chaplain. Sadly the old parson died during Staines' time in that office and neither he nor his wife was alive to see the day in 1801 when William Staines, now Sir William, duly became Lord Mayor of London.

Was the lady clairvoyant? Or did she sow a seed of ambition in the young man which bore fruit years later?

Sir William's memorial is in St Giles' church, Cripplegate, in the City of London. It would seem that it was not just Dick Whittington whose elevation to Lord Mayor was strangely foretold!

Let's Be
Rude About
Brentford

B RENTFORD, Middlesex's old county town, seems to be
one of those places that writers have to be rude
about. It seems to have gained a reputation for dirt and
disorder. In the 18th century there was a saying that a
place was 'as dirty as Old Brentford at Christmas'.
William Camden's *Britannia* in 1789 called the town
'dirty, long and ill-built'. Oliver Goldsmith and John Gay
expressed similar sentiments, Gay writing in verse of

... Brentford, tedious town
For dirty streets and white-legged chickens known

while Goldsmith, in *Citizen of the World*, described a race
'run on the road from London to a village called
Brentford, between a turnip cart, a dust-cart and a
dung-cart'. Brentford was, in former times, celebrated –
if that is the right word – for such barbaric sports as
bear-baiting.

LET'S BE RUDE ABOUT BRENTFORD

James Thorne, a Victorian writer, put it this way in 1875: 'With its long narrow High Street, back slums, factories, rough riverside and labouring population, Brentford has always borne an unenviable reputation for dirt and ill-odours. The long dreary High Street is not only dirty, but dull and monotonous, and quite devoid of interest.'

There are many who would say that this is still the case!

Brentford's reputation for disorder dates from a series of notorious election riots in the 18th century. Because of its historic status as the county town, Brentford was where the hustings and voting to elect the Members of Parliament for Middlesex took place, in the area known as The Butts, a large square formerly used for archery practice, behind the old market house. There is still a road called The Butts, just off the High Street and Half Acre in the town centre.

It is not clear when polling first took place there but from the early 1700s the Middlesex elections were held in this location and nowhere else. Very few people had the vote, of course, before the Great Reform Act of 1832, but it seems that elections were not the half-hearted or staid affairs that they are now. The crowds thronging the streets were immense and things could get quite riotous.

When John Wilkes, the radical reformer, was elected in 1768 the baying mobs in the streets took up the battle-cry 'Wilkes and Liberty', things got out of hand, rioters destroyed the poll books and one person was killed. The popularity of Wilkes was so great that all classes of his supporters went about the town bearing his picture printed on such items as punch bowls or milk jugs, plates or dishes – items that would be worth a fortune to collectors of political memorabilia had they survived.

Wilkes and his opponent Colonel Lutterell were standing together on the hustings when Wilkes quietly asked the Colonel whether he thought there were more fools or knaves among the large crowds of Wilkites below.

'I'll tell them what you say and so put an end to you at once,' said Lutterell, hoping to take advantage of his opponent's cynical contempt for his supporters. Seeing that Wilkes seemed unmoved by this threat, he asked, 'Why aren't you worried?'

'Because I would tell them that you were lying and then they would put an end to you, not me,' the wily old rabble-rouser replied!

Politics always was a dirty game. An attempt to massage the figures and manipulate the poll seems to be apparent in this letter from the Prime Minister, Lord North, to a senior judge, Sir Eardley Wilmot. Asking for Wilmot's public support for Lutterell's campaign he wrote: 'It is manifest how much it is for the honour of Parliament, and the quiet of the country in future times, that Mr Wilkes should have an antagonist at the next Brentford election. There is the greatest reason to believe that the Colonel will have a very considerable show of legal votes, nay, even a majority, if his friends are not deterred from appearing at the poll. It is the game of Mr Wilkes and his friends to increase these alarms, but they cannot frighten the candidate from his purpose; and I am very confident that the voters will run no risk. There is nothing, I imagine, that every true friend of this country must wish more than to see Mr Wilkes disappointed in his projects; and nothing, I am convinced, will defeat them more effectually than to fill up the vacant seat for Middlesex, especially if it can be done with legal votes.'

That last sentence seems to imply that he would have been prepared to see his aim achieved by illegal methods if necessary but the judge wrote back to say that 'it would be highly improper for me to interfere in any shape in that election.'

Even after the turbulent times of John Wilkes, the Brentford hustings remained notorious for their violence. In 1802 when Sir Francis Burdett was elected, one man was killed and the *Annual Register* for that year reported that 'it is impossible for any but those who have witnessed a Middlesex election to conceive the picture it exhibited: it was a continued scene of riot, disorder and tumult.'

Byron's Tomb

Ask to see Byron's tomb at Harrow School and you could cause confusion to any ill-informed tourists within earshot.

The poet Lord Byron is not buried at Harrow at all. What they will show you is the grave of John Peachey, who died in 1780. Not a famous man at all but he must have been of some significance in his day for he secured a resting-place with the finest view in Middlesex, looking out dramatically towards Windsor and beyond.

It was this view that entranced the precocious young poet with so much living to cram into a short span. He would sit on this flat-topped memorial and watch the sunset. He wrote of this

> Spot of my youth! whose hoary branches sigh,
> Swept by the breeze that fans thy cloudless sky;
> Where now alone I muse, who oft have trod,
> With those I loved, thy soft and verdant sod.
> Oh! as I trace again thy winding hill
> Mine eyes admire, my heart adores thee still.
> Here might I sleep where all my hopes arose,
> Scene of my youth, and couch of my repose.

BYRON'S TOMB

All this became known and, particularly after his death, the spot became a place of pilgrimage, rather in the way that mawkish fans follow the footsteps of pop stars who die tragically young. One of Harrow's traditional school songs tells how

> Byron lay, lazily lay,
> Hid from lesson and game away
> Dreaming poetry all alone
> Up-a-top of the Peachey stone.

Things became so bad that the grave had to be protected by iron railings and any budding poet seeking inspiration from bodily contact with the very stone that supported the Byronic behind would be faced with some difficulty. The elm tree that shaded him as he lay dreaming has gone – burned down – after a bonfire had been lit in it one 5th November during the First World War.

But there is a Byron lying close by – his little daughter, christened Clara Allegra.

Allegra was a 'love-child' in today's parlance. She was the result of an affair Byron had with Mary Shelley's step-sister in Switzerland. Her mother, perhaps feeling that Byron was not showing sufficient concern for the child or providing for her upkeep, sent Allegra to him in Venice – which may not have been foremost in his plans at all! However, he seems to have taken a proper fatherly interest and thought her 'a pretty little girl enough and reckoned like papa.' He discussed provision for her education with the Shelleys and set aside a large sum of money to pay for this.

The girl seems to have become somewhat wayward –

'obstinate as a mule and ravenous as a vulture,' he wrote, 'health good, temper tolerable but for vanity and pertinacity. She thinks herself handsome and will do as she pleases.'

When Allegra was four, perhaps afraid that he was bringing up a spoiled little madam, Byron packed her off to a convent in Ravenna. But suddenly, aged just five, the child contracted typhus fever and died. 'It is God's will; let us mention it no more,' Byron said when the news was broken to him in Pisa.

Harrow clearly was where his heart was for it was in St Mary's church, up on the hill, that Byron wished his child to be buried. He even stipulated the exact location. In a letter to a friend he wrote, 'Near the door, on the left-hand as you enter, there is a monument with a tablet containing these words:

> When sorrow weeps o'er virtue's sacred dust
> Our tears become us and our grief is just.
> Such were the tears she who grateful plays
> The last tribute of her love and praise.'

These words can still be seen on the plaque to Thomas Ryves, son-in-law to Thomas Graham, an apothecary in the time of the first two King Georges. Byron said that there was nothing particularly remarkable about this verse but he had clearly remembered it. Sitting in the Harrow boys' gallery Sunday after Sunday he had seen the words often enough and they had made an impression. 'As near it as convenient,' he wrote, 'I would wish Allegra to be buried and on the wall a marble tablet placed.'

He wanted the funeral service to be conducted by his old friend and tutor at Harrow, Henry Drury – but there was a problem: the Vicar of St Mary's refused to have the funeral held within the church. Byron's reputation was already too wicked and the child was illegitimate. Eventually the Church authorities felt it would be possible for little Allegra – who, after all, could be judged the innocent product of, not responsible for, her father's sinfulness! – to be buried in the porch outside and this is what was done.

Byron wanted some words from the Book of Samuel, 'I shall go to her, but she shall not return to me', to be put on a memorial tablet to his daughter, but again the Vicar would not allow it. Clara Allegra Byron, aged five, thus lay forgotten for over 150 years until 19th April 1980 when the Byron Society was able to place a small memorial stone to the right of the main door.

In a letter to Mary and Percy Shelley soon after Allegra's death Lord Byron wrote, 'I suppose Time will do his usual work. Death has done his.'

Held Captive
in
the Wash

❧

YOUNG girls, especially if they were at all pretty, were well advised to steer clear of Susannah Wells' lodging house at Enfield Wash, a dozen or so miles out of the city on the Hertford road. Ill-repute was putting it mildly. Once a beer-house, the way it had been run was too much for the justices even in the lax days of the 18th century. Wise parents in the straggling village kept their daughters well away from the seedy lodgings frequented by vagrants, gypsies and men who had good reason to be absent awhile from their normal low-life haunts.

Elizabeth Canning was a good girl, a demure servant at a house in Aldermanbury in the City of London. Not the kind of girl you'd find in Susannah's company, so it was quite a shock when she disappeared after a day with her aunt and uncle at Smithfield!

They felt awful afterwards and no wonder. They took her part of the way home but then left her at Aldgate, leaving her to walk the mile back to the City alone.

She was not seen again until nearly a month later.

Thomas, her mother's lodger, was there when she staggered in through the door. It made quite a tale to tell later in the tavern. 'Almost dead, she was,' he said. 'As black as that chimney stack, dressed up with an ol' bit of handkerchief round her head and a dirty ragged bed-gown that was hanging half off her!'

Her mother had jumped up from the fire which she had been staring into sightlessly for the last couple of hours. 'Lor, love, what happened to you? Where on earth have you been?'

It was a while before they could understand her through her sobbing. 'I was nearly home, Mother, in Moorfields by Bedlam Wall, when these two lusty fellows jumped me and stole my purse.' Another bout of weeping trembled through her body. 'I can't remember what happened but then I was in this lane, somewhere out in the country, being dragged along. They took me to this house and there were three women there.

'I thought they'd help me – they were women after all. "You'll be alright now, dearie," the oldest one said, "just listen to me. Do what I say and you'll soon have some fine clothes to show off your looks."'

Elizabeth broke down again at the memory. 'I saw her face, evil and leering she was. The way she touched me, feeling me all over and just looking. I knew what she expected me to do to earn those clothes and I wasn't having any of that! And she had a knife and cut the stays of my dress, threw them away and they took me upstairs and locked me in.'

News of Elizabeth's return had quickly spread among her mother's friends and neighbours. By now there was quite a crowd listening to the awful tale as she told how she had been imprisoned for four weeks in an empty garret and fed on stale bread and water.

'What happened, how did you get away?' someone asked.

'There was an old window that had been blocked up with a board,' Elizabeth said, 'I worked away at it and managed to get it loose and slid down the roof when no one was about.'

'Do you know where the house was?' asked a man called Scarratt who had been listening with increasing interest.

'Somewhere up the Hertford road, I think,' she replied ''cause I'd peeped through the boards and seen the Hertford coach go by.'

Scarratt whistled softly. 'I'll lay a guinea to a farthing she's been at Mother Wells' at Enfield Wash! Every villain from here to Cheshunt knows old Susannah and most of them have been in that house of hers an' all – and knew what they were going to get there too. You're lucky to have got out with your virtue intact, my girl!'

Soon Elizabeth's escape was the talk of every alehouse in the City and the cry went round that 'something must be done!' An officer of the Lord Mayor was dispatched to Enfield Wash with a group of men to arrest Susannah and hold her until Elizabeth could be brought to identify and accuse her. Upstairs they found a loft, not very much like the garret room she had described as her place of imprisonment but it was the only room in the house that remotely resembled it and they supposed her memory might have been confused by her ordeal.

They rounded up all the people in the house and held them for questioning. Many protested their innocence of any wrongdoing and pleaded that the affair should be kept from their wives and sweethearts!

Elizabeth was brought from London to identify the woman who had been the ringleader in her abduction and, thanks to Scarratt, Susannah Wells was the prime suspect. She was waiting with the others in the kitchen but the Mayor's officer then changed his mind and sent them all back into the room and told Elizabeth to go in and pick out her captor. Crucially when they sat down again they did not all sit where they had before. Susannah had swapped places with a gypsy woman called Mary Squires and when Elizabeth came in it was Mary, not Susannah, that she pointed to!

When Mary Squires came to trial at the Old Bailey she produced witnesses who swore she was at Abbotsbury in Dorset on the day when she was supposed to have been committing the crime at Enfield Wash. That ought to have clinched her innocence but the public demand for someone to be found guilty of this crime and the authorities' need for a conviction to placate the mob were so great that neither judge nor jury would listen and poor Mary was condemned to death.

But then, in the nick of time, new evidence came to light and even the most rabid caller for retribution had to accept that the conviction was unsafe. It turned out that Scarratt, who had first implicated Susannah, had previously lived at Enfield and had more than once availed himself of the services on offer at her shady establishment. It was suggested that he might well have had a grudge against her and wanted her out of the way. Perhaps he knew what Elizabeth herself had been up to during that fateful month – was she as innocent as she seemed and was Scarratt able to blackmail her into telling a false tale of abduction and imprisonment?

Had he perhaps primed Elizabeth, telling her where

Susannah had been sitting for the 'identification parade', only for his cunning plan to be foiled by the intervention of the Mayor's officer?

When this new evidence and the doubts of Scarratt's trustworthiness became known, the Lord Mayor petitioned the Crown to reopen the case, pleading that the public hysteria surrounding it had prevented Mary from having a fair trial. She was indeed acquitted and Elizabeth Canning now found herself in the dock rather than the witness box and charged with perjury.

This time she was not believed. Her story was found wanting.

'Was it likely,' the prosecution argued, 'that two muggers would, after robbing her, take the risk of dragging her unconscious to a lonely house miles away, instead of simply making good their escape with the money? Would anyone trying to lure a pretty young woman into prostitution, on whose immoral earnings they hoped to live, starve her so that she lost all her allure and attraction?'

Elizabeth was found guilty and sentenced to be transported to penal servitude in Britain's American colonies – this was in the days before Australia became used for this purpose.

It must have been an awful experience for Elizabeth Canning – held on a convict ship with all manner and classes of felons; a young woman at the mercy of bored, disinterested or sadistic guards and exposed to nameless dangers and exploitation. She was never able to return home and died in Connecticut in 1773, twenty years after the mysterious events that changed her life for ever.

So Elizabeth Canning, possibly the victim of cruel kidnap and imprisonment, possibly of blackmail and perhaps the demure innocent she first appeared, ended her days in a faraway land of which she knew little. Her story sounded so plausible, similar things have happened in our own days, but we also know that evidence can be misleading or manipulated. Things are not always what they appear to be.

Wilberforce's
Last Battle

WILLIAM Wilberforce is, of course, nationally known for his long and successful campaigning against the slave trade. In his declining years and after all those battles, he might have hoped for a quiet life when he moved to the rural village of Mill Hill in the early 1830s – but a rather unedifying row with the combative Vicar of Hendon, Rev Theodore Williams, meant that this was not to be.

Wilberforce's new home at Highwood Hill was three miles from the parish church of St Mary's in Hendon. His neighbours were wearily familiar with this journey Sunday by Sunday but Wilberforce decided to do something about it. His first plan was to build a private chapel on his own land but a local landowner, Sir Charles Flower, then offered him a plot of land for a new church for the whole village. There was a lot of support for the idea, not least from the government and church authorities who were keen on supporting such 'Proprietory Chapels' to meet the needs of the growing population and to counter pro-revolutionary fervour spreading from Europe.

But they had reckoned without the Reverend Williams.

The issue was partly theological. Wilberforce was a leading member of the growing Evangelical wing of the Church of England whereas Williams' stance was more traditional. But it also has to be said that Williams feared for the pew rents he obtained from the wealthy folk from Mill Hill, families who even maintained coach houses at Church End, Hendon, to house their carriages during Sunday services. He was himself a wealthy man whose inherited fortune had come from the profits of the very slave trade that Wilberforce had fought against.

Rev Theodore Williams was an abrasive and litigious man. A dispute between the Vicar and the Parish Vestry meeting over the issue of setting the local rate had led to a near brawl when the members of the Vestry unprecedently attempted to charge Williams a rate payment for the vicarage. Williams had caused the offending Vestrymen to be summoned and fined heavily. There were other occasions on which he was involved in law suits against individual parishioners. There was, however, a gentler side to his character. His garden at the vicarage, which he had created (with the help of several gardeners!) was widely admired as a model of what could be achieved on a one and a half acre site.

This was the man that William Wilberforce had unwittingly taken on. Williams bitterly opposed the plan for the Proprietory Chapel at Mill Hill. He wrote a series of letters to the Bishop of London in an attempt to prevent the work starting.

But Wilberforce had powerful allies in the locality, including such eminent men as Sir Stanford Raffles of Singapore fame, as well as the support of the Bishop and the church was built and opened as St Paul's in 1833. Even then Williams did not give up. He produced affidavits from the builders stating that the 250,000 bricks used in its construction were inferior and claimed that this was due to nepotism as Wilberforce had set up one of his sons as a brickmaker on his own lands (where there was an old brickworks). He may even have been right because in the next hundred years or so the congregation of St Paul's faced frequent and large bills for the repair of the fabric! In the 1860s disagreements about the church and its suitability for worship – such as the pews not allowing space for worshippers to kneel – a posture which its Evangelical builders had considered dangerously Popish – nearly led to its demolition.

Sadly Wilberforce died in 1833, just before the church's consecration, but St Paul's, Mill Hill still survives as a memorial to his last and successful battle.

The Battle
of
Liverpool Street

❧

RIOTS at railway stations do not happen all that often, despite all the indignities that rail commuters have to suffer – but the Battle of Liverpool Street which took place early in 1899 could be considered an exception.

The construction of Liverpool Street station in the 1870s had involved the demolition of several streets of poor working-class houses. Part of the special Act of Parliament that allowed this was the proviso that the Great Eastern Railway should provide cheap workmen's fares on some early trains on selected lines into the suburbs so that artisans displaced by the new station could afford the longer journey into London. One of these routes was the line out to Edmonton and Enfield.

Now this was all very well but the Great Eastern Railway Company was reluctant to sully its trains with riff-raff and severely restricted the number of trains on which these cheap tickets were valid.

Demand rapidly outstripped supply and there was

severe overcrowding. Things had got so bad that on 24th January 1899 the doors of Lower Edmonton station had had to be closed because nobody else could be squeezed onto the platform. The last two workmen's trains, the 6.17 am and the 6.21 am, left grossly overloaded. Those locked-out missed their trains and many did not have enough money to travel on the more expensive later ones.

Something had to be done and in the true spirit of eminent Victorians they set up a committee. With the resounding title of the Edmonton Workmen's Train Association and led by a group of local councillors and clergymen this organization badgered the GER until the railway company took action.

Unfortunately, as is the way with these things, the action that they took only made things worse. From now on, it was announced, tickets for these so-called Parliamentary Trains would have to be pre-booked, valid only on one nominated train and with a limit of just 750 from Lower Edmonton to Liverpool Street.

This was nowhere near enough and on the first morning of the new scheme a large crowd of resentful ticketless workmen appeared outside the station from which they had been barred. They had a choice – they had either to pay the full fare (which most could not afford) or they would lose a day's pay if they could not get to work.

This was no choice at all and the angry mob stormed the ticket barrier and crowded onto the 6.21. Clearly there was going to be trouble when they got to Liverpool Street! An argument with the ticket-collectors at the terminus led to three arrests.

But this was small fry compared to the following day when the same scenario was enacted. This time though the Edmonton men staged a protest meeting when they got to Liverpool Street. This soon degenerated into a running battle across the crowded station concourse. About 2,000 workmen attempted to rescue one of their number who had been taken into custody for fare evasion. A Railway Police Officer was set upon and badly beaten up before he could be rescued by his outnumbered colleagues.

On the third day, much the same thing happened again and the protesters pelted police and ticket collectors with the contents of their lunchboxes.

Such a situation could not be allowed to continue and the GER was prevailed upon to relax the restrictions and to provide additional workmen's trains from Lower Edmonton before seven o'clock in the morning.

Even so, for many years to come travel on the old Parliamentary Trains from Enfield and Edmonton to the metropolis was an overcrowded and probably unsavoury experience.

Handel's
Harmonious
Blacksmith

❧

THE sky darkened threateningly and the rain was
falling harder. In Edgware High Street the musician,
new tunes that had been running round his head
temporarily forgotten, scampered for shelter. The door
of the blacksmith's forge on the west side of the street
stood open and he gratefully stepped inside.

William Powell, the smith, a fine-looking man, nearly
six feet in height, hardly paused in his work. Clean
shirtsleeves rolled up his muscular arms, collar thrown
back loose on his broad shoulders, he sang as he
continued hammering. It was a beautiful melody,
chiming in exactly with the tone emitted by the anvil as
the blows struck it.

George Frederick Handel, for this was the musician
who had sought shelter, was transfixed by the sound
and that moment in 1721 became the inspiration for
one of his most famous pieces of music, much-loved to
this day. The blacksmith told his delighted visitor that

he had heard the tune long ago but did not know who had composed it. Handel, so the story goes, kept humming the tune to himself until he got back to Canons, the great house at Little Stanmore where he was employed as Kappellmeister, and elaborated the theme into the piece we know today.

Canons' owner at the time, James Brydges, Duke of Chandos, had created a home that during its brief existence became a byword for courtly magnificence. He made his fortune as Paymaster General to the Duke of Marlborough from 1707 to 1712, during which time he amassed the grand sum of £600,000 – a fortune in those days. Through his wife Mary he inherited the Canons estate which was named after its original owners, the Priory of St Bartholomew the Great. The best architects money could buy were employed and between 1713 and 1725 a house arose that Defoe described as 'the most magnificent in England'. Not only the best architects but also the best painters and the finest musicians – which is how G.F. Handel came to be living in this part of rural Middlesex.

St Laurence, Whitchurch, the parish church of Little Stanmore and Canons, was rebuilt by the Duke in the same florid style, featuring fine paintings and an organ-case carved by Grinling Gibbons. Attached to the organ a brass plate recalls that Handel composed the oratorio *Esther* on it. There is a grandiose mausoleum where the Duke and his successive wives are interred and also a memorial to William Powell, the Harmonious Blacksmith himself. This stone, which bears in a sunken medallion a hammer, anvil, laurel wreath and a bar of music, records his name and date of death, 27th February 1780, aged 78. It adds that 'he was parish clerk during the time the immortal Handel was organist of this church.'

Well before his death William Powell would have seen the family at Canons fall on hard times. In 1744 the Duke's son, deeply in debt, was forced to sell but could only raise £11,000 for what had cost a quarter of a million merely 25 years before.

Sadly for us, musicologists and historians have poured scorn on much of this pretty story. William Powell, they say, was not even apprenticed to a smith until 1725, four years after Handel is alleged to have sheltered in his forge. Even the claim that Handel composed *Esther* at the Whitchurch organ is disputed for he had no need to be playing an organ during composition. It would in any event have been more convenient to use the one at Canons.

Moreover the details of Handel's life are still quite obscure but it seems that he was living abroad for much of the time when he was supposed to be employed at Canons. Even if he was in the Duke's service, they say, he would much more likely have lived at one of the family's London houses. All that can be said is that he may well have played on the old organ in the church at some time during his employment. It would be odd if he had not.

This tale, which Arthur Mee describes as 'a gathering snowball of falsehood', began when a writer to *The Times* started the legend of the forge in the storm. It seems that two local men with an eye to the lucrative tourist trade made up the link with William Powell – who really did exist – and organized the subscription fund for a wooden memorial in the church, later replaced by gullible parishoners in 1868 with the one we see today!

According to Handel's biographer, Newman Flower, there was a blacksmith's apprentice in Bath, a young man called William Lintern, who became so fond of the tune that he sang it all the time until his friends nicknamed him 'The Harmonious Blacksmith', after which the tune acquired the nickname. It seems it was merely one of the pieces Handel used to write for his royal pupils, one of a set he published during his time at Canons.

Yet so often these picturesque legends do contain a grain of truth and the great composer must have had some links with the Duke of Chandos and the palace at Canons. *Esther*, for which he received £1,000 from the Duke, was certainly performed at Whitchurch in 1721 with the great man himself present.

On 25th September 1790 a Grand Concert of Handel's Sacred Music was performed at Whitchurch, including anthems composed by him at Canons. The profits were intended for the benefit of the Sunday schools in adjoining parishes but the event was not a financial success. It seems that the Master's musical heritage was no longer appreciated by the locals!

Hendon's Air Pioneer

STANDING proudly in the great British tradition of coming second, pioneer aviator Claude Grahame-White first came to public notice by not quite winning the £10,000 prize put up by the *Daily Mail* in 1910 for the first flight between London and Manchester. Thwarted by engine trouble and bad weather he was pipped to the post in April of that year by a French pilot named Paulhan, but not before an epic and valiant attempt which saw Grahame-White flying through the night, guided only by the headlights of cars and the signal lamps of the railway!

Despite his defeat, he became a national hero and later that year he purchased a tract of land at Hendon (from which ironically his rival had taken off) with the intention of establishing the first London Aerodrome. The following year the first UK Airmails were flown from Hendon to Windsor and there was brave talk of Hendon becoming 'the Clapham Junction or Crewe of the Universe'!

Regular air displays were established and for a time

before the First World War became social events to rival Ascot, Epsom and Henley! Local people flocked to watch the fun, many taking up vantage points on nearby slopes where the flying could be watched free of charge.

It was all so new and so exciting – loops were looped, usually successfully, but there were enough thrills and spills to satisfy the disaster-seekers. A 'Flying Fete' held in 1912 included planes equipped with powerful searchlights, powered by accumulators fitted internally, following a one and a half mile circuit lit up from pylons. Below were enclosures and a bandstand decorated with coloured lanterns. It must have been a fine sight on a warm Middlesex evening but did perhaps the display of fire balloons and fireworks representing 'War in the Air' awaken grim forebodings in the more thoughtful onlookers?

When war did come in 1914 Claude Grahame-White founded the aviation company which bore his name to manufacture military aircraft. It became the focus of a major engineering industry and hitherto-rural Colindale was transformed in a few months. Grahame-White became a national hero all over again but later everything went horribly wrong for this stalwart pioneer.

Just before the end of the war the Grahame-White aviation company had been given government orders for hundreds more aircraft which then were not needed. The contracts were cancelled and, despite an attempt to diversify into manufacturing motor-cars and furniture, the firm was ruined. In 1922 the Treasury took possession of the factory and the staff were discharged. A long legal battle followed and eventually Grahame-White received fair compensation.

Hendon Aerodrome became an RAF station and the

home of the air displays that thrilled so many in the interwar years – but that dream of Hendon as the hub of the world's air transport network proved an illusion, a dream realised after the Second World War by the expansion of Heath Row aerodrome, to the dubious benefit of beleaguered West Middlesex!

Archbishop
for a Week

A PLAQUE on the west wall of St Mary's church at Ealing commemorates Thomas Bradwardine, a former Vicar of the parish, the most short-lived Archbishop of Canterbury in the 1,400 year history of that ancient office. Struck down by the Black Death in July 1349 within hours of his return to England after his consecration, he was Archbishop for barely a week.

Thomas Bradwardine was born and brought up in Sussex, but nothing is known of his life before he went up to Oxford in the early years of the 14th century, becoming one of the first scholars of the newly-established Merton College.

He was clearly a hugely-talented academic and soon became well known, not just as a theologian but also as a mathematician, astronomer and moral philosopher. At the request of the fellows of Merton College he delivered a series of theological lectures, later expanded into a book which remained influential for centuries.

His subject was the vexed one of the extent of man's free will compared to God's knowing all that must come to pass, and when the subject comes up in Chaucer's *Canterbury Tales* in the Nun's Priest's Tale we read:

> But I me cannot boult it to the bren
> As can the holy doctour Saint Austin
> Or Boece, or the Bishop Bradwardyn

in other words, 'it's too complicated for me – only folk like St Augustine or Bishop Bradwardine can understand it.'

A man of Thomas's brains and high social standing was bound to go far in the medieval Church. His patron was another Sussex man, Roger of Bury, Bishop of Durham and Chancellor of England. Bishop Roger surrounded himself with a large retinue of esquires and chaplains, partly from a love of their company and splendour, but also from appreciation of the society of learned men who could help him in the formation of a grand library.

Through Roger's influence, Thomas Bradwardine was appointed Chancellor of St Paul's Cathedral and with this came the living of the remote little country village of Ealing. How much time he had to spare for his parochial duties must be doubtful for, in addition to his other responsibilities, he was soon appointed one of King Edward III's chaplains. This took him overseas on the King's campaigns during the 1340s and he was in attendance upon the King at the Battle of Crécy and the capture of Calais from the French. His sermons were so stirring and his prayers so fervent that many attributed the English successes to his persuasive powers with the Almighty.

When the old Archbishop Stratford died in August 1348, Thomas Bradwardine was the natural choice and he was duly nominated by the Pope. Although he was clearly the right man for the job, his appointment was not without controversy. It was a time of great political turmoil in Europe and in the Church and the Pope's position was to a large extent dependent upon the support of the King of England. So much so that the Pope had been heard to remark bitterly that if the English King were to ask him to appoint a jackass as Archbishop of Canterbury, he would have to comply.

A dissident group of Cardinals took this comment too seriously. In the middle of a splendid banquet held by the Pope in the new Archbishop's honour in Avignon, the doors of the banqueting hall were thrown open and a clown entered, seated on a jackass, and made a mock plea to be made the next Archbishop of Canterbury!

This jape caused the authorities much embarrassment in view of Thomas's erudition and learning. The offenders were soundly rebuked by the Pope and Bradwardine was consecrated Archbishop on 13th July 1349.

It was now that Thomas Bradwardine showed himself to be either a very brave or a very foolhardy man. Although he knew that the fearsome plague was raging throughout England, he immediately hurried there from France. He landed at Dover on 19th August and did homage to the King at Eltham Palace on the 22nd, from which date his position as Archbishop was confirmed legally. From Eltham, then in rural Kent, he made the short journey to London where he was to lodge at the Lambeth residence of the Bishop of Rochester.

The next morning he felt feverish but there was no great alarm as he attributed this to fatigue after his journey – although perhaps he secretly suspected the

119

worst. Soon there could be no doubt as the dreaded tumours under his arms made their appearance. He died on 26th August and, despite the obvious risks, his body was taken to Canterbury for burial in his cathedral.

How much this brave, learned and saintly man saw of the Ealing parish which still honours him we may never know. Certainly he would not recognise St Mary's church, rebuilt on several occasions since his day, most recently in Victorian times, resulting in an exterior of ponderous ugliness and a glittering mock Byzantine interior.

But perhaps he would be touched that his name is still remembered on the hallowed ground that once owed him respect, long before Ealing earned her 20th century title as Queen of the Suburbs!

Slow Train
to Shepperton

❧

NOBODY wants a motorway built past their front door and in Victorian times the coming of the railway was often seen in the same way. All over the country there were great battles between the promoters of new lines – out for a good profit – and those local residents and landowners who did not want these nasty smelly new-fangled steam trains anywhere near them, thank you very much! The proprietors of Eton College, for example, did all they could to stop the building of the line from Slough to Windsor.

It was 1860 and in the quaint and isolated riverside village of Shepperton, the Lord of the Manor, William Schaw Lindsay MP, had a problem. He was an active Member of Parliament, but he was having great difficulty actually getting to Westminster. It should have been quite easy – driven by his coachman from his home by the river, acknowledging the respectful greetings of the villagers, then across the bridge at Walton and on to the station where he could travel up to Waterloo in First Class comfort and privacy.

SUNBURY

SHEPPERTON

SLOW TRAIN TO SHEPPERTON

But in 1859 Walton Bridge, a notoriously precarious structure, had collapsed. Its impoverished owners showed no sign of starting rebuilding work and those wishing to cross were obliged to entrust their lives to a lumbering punt.

Naturally the infuriated Lindsay soon made his feelings known: 'In dark winter nights and during floods,' he wrote, 'this mode of conveyance is positively dangerous, but Surrey and Middlesex have to submit to it. The two wealthiest counties in the world have no other means of communication.'

Lindsay was not the sort of man to suffer inconvenience placidly. Born in Ayr in 1816, he had been orphaned at the age of six and brought up by his uncle, a non-conformist minister. Determined to seek fame and fortune on the high seas, he eventually worked his passage to Liverpool by labouring in the coal-hole of a steamer. Arriving there friendless and destitute he was unemployed for two months, wandering the wharves and docks exhausted and starving, sleeping in sheds or under the stars.

At length he obtained a berth as a cabin-boy on the *Isabella*, a West Indiaman. This was the start of a climb to Second Mate, Mate, Chief Mate and ultimately Captain of the good ship *Olive Branch* in a career that included more than one shipwreck and an encounter with pirates in the Persian Gulf. In 1839 he retired from the sea and settled in Hartlepool as an agent for a coal company. A self-made man in the grand Victorian manner, he became one of the largest shipowners in the country and MP for Tynemouth in 1854. In 1856 he purchased the manor of Shepperton, residing in some style in the fine old manor house next to the Thames.

Finding no response to his campaign for repairs to be

started on the bridge, this energetic parliamentarian conceived the idea of promoting a railway from Shepperton to London, ignoring the contemptuous remark of one local farmer that 'a donkey cart would take all the goods and passengers that go between London and Shepperton in a month!'

Nor were the residents of nearby Sunbury of much help. They offered an 'abundance of advice but no pecuniary assistance,' Lindsay complained, and objected most vociferously to the proposed route that would have brought the line close to their village. They managed to get the plans altered, diverting the route northwards so that Sunbury station was built in the bleak wastelands of Sunbury Common. 'The villagers of Sunbury would not have the station where the promoters wished it to be, close to the village, but sent it three-quarters of a mile from their doors,' he said. 'I dare say that on a wet morning or dark winter's night many of the good people of Sunbury now wish the station was a little nearer to their firesides.'

One man who suffered more than most from the change in plans was the unfortunate entrepreneur who bought a plot of land next to the original site for Sunbury station and built a pub to cater for the thirst of railway passengers. By the time the pub, named the Railway Arms, had been built, the proposed route had been changed and the station was to be half a mile to the north but it bore its inappropriate name for around a century, before being renamed the Admiral Hawke in 1968.

Lindsay's railway opened in 1864. Shepperton station was almost as remote from its village as Sunbury and the line was later described by one critic as crossing 'a flat and somewhat dreary region of Middlesex to terminate, to all seeming, in a potato field as if weary of going further into such country.' The writer was Father W.J. Scott, an eccentric Anglo-Catholic priest, Vicar of St Saviour's church, Upper Sunbury and a Director of the Great Western Railway!

The stalwart MP was unrepentant. He said that he had 'no interest whatever in the line going one yard beyond our village.'

Any plans there might have been to extend the railway beyond Shepperton to Chertsey were quietly abandoned and the Shepperton branch settled down to become eventually a slightly quirky appendix to the Southern suburban network. However, there is a little twist to this story, provided by a rogue early morning arrival from Waterloo in April 1982 which made a brave attempt to bring to fruition the plans for an extension by failing to stop on arrival at Shepperton station and crashing through the buffers at the end of the line. No one was hurt but the train ended up by mounting the wall at the end of the track and coming to rest poised precariously above the traffic lights at the crossroads at the end of the High Street.

Lest We Forget

LONG after its great days in the 17th century, Harefield Park was owned by an Australian with the somewhat improbable name of Billyard Leake. In 1915, as the grim roll-call of casualties from the battlefields of the First World War began to increase, he offered the estate to the government of his homeland to serve as a hospital for Aussie soldiers for the duration of the conflict.

It was well-used. Thousands of injured men found rest and recovery there but sadly 111 soldiers and one nursing sister did not return home.

A piece of Harefield's churchyard was set aside as a burial ground. The first soldier's funeral was as sad as all that followed. The Union Jack belonging to the nearby school was used to cover the young man's coffin and this practice continued.

After the war this flag was sent to Adelaide High School as a memento. The school sent Harefield a new Union Jack and also an Australian flag. In 1921 identical headstones and a memorial were put up. April 25th, Anzac Day, is marked by the children from Harefield School who lay flowers on every grave and hold a service.

LEST WE FORGET

A few miles away in the cemetery in Chestnut Avenue, Northwood, there is the grave of another Australian who never made it home, the journalist Edward Honey.

His claim to be remembered lies in the fact that it was Honey who had the idea of the Two Minutes Silence to commemorate those who had fallen in the war. The idea came to him in the unlikely setting of a Fleet Street tea shop.

Honey wrote an article outlining his idea which was read by Sir Percy Fitzpatrick of the South African government. The idea was taken up in South Africa first but Fitzpatrick passed it on to King George V who invited Honey to Buckingham Palace.

Mr Honey lived to see his idea implemented in England but sadly died just before the second Armistice Day. After the Second World War the observance was moved from 11th November to the nearest Sunday, a change disapproved of by many. In recent years the period of silence in shops and workplaces just before 11 am on the eleventh day of the eleventh month seems to have experienced something of a revival for a new generation.

Edward Honey would doubtless approve.